D0615159

No More Excuses:
Black Men Stand Up!

No More Excuses:
Black Men Stand Up!

Robert Jackson

To: Mason
Keep God First!

Robert Jackson

L P

Lavelle Publishing

Lavelle Publishing

P.O. Box 29512

Indianapolis, IN 46229-0512

Published by Lavelle Publishing

First Printing May 2008

No More Excuses: Black Men Stand Up

Copyright © 2008 by Robert Jackson

All Rights Reserved

ISBN 13   978-0-9659254-1-2

ISBN 10   0-9659254-1-2

LCCN   2008904627

Printed in the United States of America

Designed by Tajuana TJ Butler

Without limiting the rights under copyright reserved above, no part of this publication may be reproduced, stored in or introduced into a retrieval system, or transmitted, in any form, or by any means (electronic, mechanical, photocopying, recording, or otherwise), without the prior written permission of both the copyright owner and the above publisher of this book.

The scanning, uploading, and distribution of this book via the Internet or via any other means without the permission of the publisher is illegal and punishable by law.

While the author has made every effort to provide accurate telephone numbers and Internet addresses at the time of publication, neither the publisher nor the author assumes any responsibility for errors, or for changes that occur after publication. Further, the publisher does not have any control over and does not assume any responsibility for author or third-party Web sites or their content.

TABLE OF CONTENT

DEDICATION

This book is dedicated in the memory of some good men close to me that I lost along my journey to find myself:

My cousin Gary Branch (1969-2006)
My childhood friend Larry Shotwell (1971-1995)
My friend/frat brother Tye "Binky" Smith (1970-1995)
My childhood friend Tony Binion (1973-1988)
My student athlete William Gooch (1984-2008)
My mentor Ralph Dowe (Wheeler's Boys/Girls Club) (1942-2005)

You will always live in my heart. May each of you rest in peace.

If you're not part of the
SOLUTION
you're part of the
PROBLEM

INTRODUCTION

Black Men Becoming Extinct

In the U.S. Black men are dying at an alarming rate. The December 1, 2007 *Newsweek* Article titled "The Search for Thugs" by Raina Kelley stated that "black males ages fifteen to nineteen died by homicide at 46 times the rate of white males their age. A large number of young men are not expecting to graduate from high school or go to college because they don't plan on making it to their 21st birthday.

As a teenager, I felt the same way. Why wouldn't I? One of my best friends Tony Binion was killed. He was only fifteen years old. He was an innocent bystander at a party and caught a bullet in his chest and died on the scene. I was only sixteen years old, but I remember like yesterday. There were a lot of young people at his funeral. Although Tony looked peaceful, the reality of him lying there at such a young age was a nightmare for me. It hurt me so bad. I cried my eyes out. He wasn't a drug dealer either. He loved going to school and was fun to be around.

After Tony was killed, my friends started dropping like flies. It seemed like I was attending a funeral every week. I did what I could to deal with the pain, but I didn't start healing until I was encouraged to speak about my experiences with all the deaths of my friends. I was in high school and spoke to middle and elementary school students about what I had gone through to help them to cope with the losses they may one day encounter. I continued sharing that message during my college years.

After the NFL didn't work out for me, I decided to teach high school. I figured there would be more young men who experienced what I went through and I wanted to be there to help them cope with their daily challenges. I found that many were trying to manage dealing with the loss of their close friends, who like me had a hard time focusing on getting their education with all the negativity and peer pressure that surrounded them. It was very therapeutic for me to cope with my past by assisting other young men with their present pains.

During my second year of teaching I was speaking to my drafting class about some of the pitfalls I faced growing up and how it seemed like our young black men were getting worse, not better. While I was speaking, one of my students, who rarely came to class, strutted in quietly as if he were invisible. He didn't make a scene, but walked slowly with his normal swagger. As usual, he had on the latest in fashions, fresh pressed Sean John Jeans and a collared shirt. His watch and platinum chain glistened.

I really never figured out his pattern. Sometimes he would be in my class every day for a week straight, then he would go missing in action for two weeks. When I looked up at him, he smiled back at me as if to say, "Let me slide today, Mr. Jackson."

I said, "I don't think so. You owe me fifty."

He turned around and dropped to the floor without saying a word and proceeded to do his pushups. I was surprised because I had expected him to walk out of class instead of cooperating. He did them quickly like he was in the military. He was pretty strong and I often wondered why he didn't play on any of the sports teams at the school. He didn't have a muscular build, but looks can be deceiving.

His actions were odd to me, because two weeks prior he had refused to do his pushups when he had come in. This time was different. It seemed as if he really cared. After he did his push ups, he said, "What are we working on today?"

We had been working on drafting and getting ready to do a special project. He had his pencils ready and went to his desk and began to work after he picked up the assignment from my desk. Other kids smirked because like me no one knew what to expect from him on any given day. He buried his nose into his paper until he was done with the assignment. He said, "I'm all done Mr. Jackson. I got skills don't I?"

I said, "Yes you do, but it would be nice if you were here more often to use those skills."

I told him how talented he was and how great he would be if he would just come to class and apply himself. He told me, "Mr. Jackson, I don't need school. I'm paid already. This school stuff isn't for me."

He began to explain how he was making good money and coming to class hindered him from getting paid. I shared with him how important it was to get his education and how it would prepare him for his adult life. He pulled out a thick roll of money, 20's, 50's and 100 dollar bills and said, "This is all I need. This is what the ladies like." He snickered with an air of confidence.

I explained to him how many of my friends thought the same way he did and how they didn't live to make it out of their 20's. I told him he was thinking like a fool, not the smart young man that I knew he was. I also reminded him that the women were only attracted to his bank roll and not him. He said, "I know, but it's still fun."

I laughed. It was funny to me, but deep down I knew he was headed toward a dead end and nothing was going to stop him from hitting that brick wall. This young man was very likable among his peers, a big comedian, making jokes out of anything. He had a great sense of humor, yet he was a very honest young man and very confident. You could see it in the way he walked into a room. The other students respected him.

I explained to him that if he continued to chase after the fast money, he would end up dead or in prison. I shared with him again how I had seen many people go the route he was going and none of them won. After listening attentively, he told me, "That's not going to happen to me..."

The bell rang and he hopped up and walked out into the hallway with his cool swagger.

We had our talks from time to time and he would constantly let me know that he was doing fine and that the dope game was not going to defeat him. He always talked as if he had it all figured out. He insisted that he trusted the people in his circle. I was frustrated because he had no idea what he was up against. I had seen first hand how drugs and money destroyed families, friendships and lives. He was naive to the fact that it could happen to him also.

After receiving his report card, he came to my class and asked me to change his grade to passing. I explained to him that the school policy stated that if he had more than five unexcused absences, he would automatically flunk class and that he had well over twenty.

"You have to earn your grades and come to class like everyone else." I said. "The only way to pass is to come to class and do the work everyday like everyone else."

He said, "I'm out of here," and walked out. That was the last time I saw him in class.

Almost five years had gone by and I was riding my motorcycle one day down 38th street in Indianapolis, a high traffic area. I stopped at a red light as another motorcycle pulled up next to me. It was him and I smiled because I was happy to run into him. He was his normal self, joking as usual. The first thing he said to me was, "Mr. Jackson, I'm still here."

I laughed with him and said, "Yes you are."

It was a bright sunny afternoon, the perfect day for riding. He checked out my bike and smiled giving me his approval. "Wow nice bike. I didn't know you rode," he said.

"So, what have you been up to over the past five years," I asked him.

He said, "You already know," smiling back to me. He was still up to the same thing, running the streets and making that fast money.

About a month later, I was hanging out with some friends at a Sports Bar and one of his classmates came up to me. He said, "Did you hear about home-boy?"

I said, "Hear what?"

He began to tell me how this young man was murdered in his own driveway after being robbed by some guys he knew. While they were attacking him, he tried to pull his gun out to defend himself, but was shot several times in the chest. He died on the scene.

I was overwhelmed with pain and emotion. I couldn't believe what I was hearing. I had just run into him and when he rode off on his bike he smiled back at me. I guess I had convinced myself that this young man was going to be okay and had beaten the odds. That bad news changed my mood and I couldn't enjoy my time out with my friends. I didn't even have the opportunity to pay my respects at his funeral because I found out too late. He was only 23 years old.

I continued to think about all the talks we had and why he didn't get the message. Was there something wrong with my message? I had told him about all my friends who were murdered and those who went to prison to serve long sentences, but sometimes you don't learn until it happens to you or someone close to you. I spoke to other young men about the same thing and they listened. Maybe I should have been more specific and spent more time teaching him how to make better choices.

His death motivated me to create workshops teaching young men about how to cope with peer pressure and make better decisions. I wanted to teach them self-discipline, self-control and responsibility. I carried my message into schools and other venues that I felt would benefit from my words.

Years later I have seen the fruits of my labor. Young men who seemed hopeless with no direction when I first met them, come up to me today thanking me for giving them good advice and for holding them accountable. Wherever I go, whether it's the mall or a restaurant, I run into young men whom are now adults whose lives I've helped change. Many of them are married, college graduates, or just hard working individuals making a positive difference in society. Some of them even decided to work with youth and give back to their communities.

There are so many young black men like the young man I spoke of earlier who deserve access to the proper tools to make the right choices in their lives. Our young men are lost and misguided and need direction. A lot of them will end up in some or all of the situations mentioned in this book at some point in their lives. Although some are smart and outgoing, others lose their focus and fall victim to making bad decisions. They need to hear from other men who have gone through similar situations, but found a way to rise above the cycle of hopelessness.

This cycle can only be stopped if black men decide collectively in our minds that enough is enough. Aren't you tired of turning to the news just to find out that another young man has been found dead and no one has any idea who his killer is? It's getting worst by the day.

It's time to stand up and take responsibility for our actions. Our women have been taking care of us long enough and although they deserve respect and praise for their efforts, it's our responsibility as men to lead our families, not theirs. It is my hope that this book will inspire you to stand up and take responsibility. Even if you were dealt bad cards, you will have an opportunity for a breakthrough and you have to be ready and prepared for it because it may never come again.

INTRODUCTION

Each of us was dealt a set of circumstances that we have to play out and sometimes we are going to make mistakes. I have made many mistakes and continue to learn from them.

As men it is our responsibility to assist the young brothers who are coming up behind us headed down the same path of destruction. Some brothers are quick to blame the "white man" or someone else for their failures. Don't get me wrong, sometimes it is the "white man" trying to hold you down, but it's up to you whether you want to remain down or not. We must focus on real solutions like furthering our education, gaining employment and making better decisions.

In My Hood

I grew up in Brightwood, a small low-income, crime filled community in Indianapolis. My mom raised five kids on her own and I was the only boy. It wasn't easy growing up in a house with four sisters. They always had each other, but I would sometimes find myself feeling very lonely because I didn't have another male to relate to, argue with or just hang out with.

I didn't have a father growing up and never met my biological father. My sisters and I all had different fathers. My baby sister is the only one out of the five of us that actually knew and had a relationship with her father. My other siblings and I had no idea where our real fathers were or who they were.

Even though the men who helped to bring us into this world were absent, my mom held down our household working two to three jobs to take care of us. She always stressed the importance of hard work and education even though she was denied hers growing up in the south in Mississippi. Times were hard when we were kids, but we made it work. We appreciated the small things. When mom brought home White Castles or pizza or Churches Chicken®, we thought it was a special occasion. She fought to keep us out of public housing, but my sisters and I spent a lot of time there since our grandmother and aunts who kept us lived there.

I don't recall many of my friends growing up with their fathers either. Maybe you're dealing with the anger of not having yours at home. Maybe you never had a conversation with him and it hurts. Maybe when he does come around, it's only for a short period of time. Even though it makes us angry, as men, we have to find other alternatives to our anger about his absence. Speaking from personal experience, it's tough dealing with that pain, but there is power in prayer. You are not measured by your biological father's presence in your life. Your real father is your creator, so you are never without one. I had to learn that for myself.

I spent many days sitting on my steps in front of my house waiting on a miracle. I thought he was going to drive up one day in a big Cadillac and take me to get some ice cream, but it never happened. Sports eventually became my escape from dealing with my pains of growing up fatherless in poverty. I stayed busy and occupied, but that hurt lingered inside me for several years.

Making Excuses

It was tough carrying that pain for so long. Making excuses only worsened my problems. When I got angry about something, I made excuses for my attitude and my actions. When I got kicked out of school, I made the excuse that I was being treated unfairly. If I didn't do well on one of my tests, I made the excuse that I did not have the proper learning environment. I tended to make excuses about everything I didn't complete or did wrong, even as an adult, until I realized that it was me who was making bad decisions and I had only my self to blame. I wasn't utilizing the gifts that God had blessed me with. Instead, I made excuses.

Everyone has been blessed with a gift. Some of us utilize them and some of us don't. Football took me all the way to the Minnesota Vikings training camp in 1995; however some of my friends who should have become NBA or NFL superstars, doctors and lawyers or engineers, fell victim to the violent streets we grew up in.

I remember one of my high school teachers saying to me, "You won't amount to anything." He said I wasn't good enough to play with the best high school players, and told me to stop worrying about going to college because I wouldn't be able to compete with other college football players and wouldn't be able to keep up my grades. I used his negative words as motivation. I refused to believe him and graduated from college with a degree in Industrial Technology. I started four years in football and made it all the way to the NFL.

Another issue that this book addresses is the cycle of irresponsibility, including destroying ourselves with the selling and usage of illegal drugs and with the participation in criminal acts. Too many intelligent brothers are locked behind bars. According to a study, in 1980 143,000 black men were in jail or prison, but by 2000 that number jumped to 791,600 and the number is still rising.

Don't wait until you get sentenced to prison to wake up. It's too late by then. I've heard criminals complain, "I had to do what I had to do to take care of my family." Maybe so, but at what point does taking care of the needs of one's family include robbing, stealing and killing?

I haven't lived a perfect life and I have paid for things I have done in the past, but at the end of the day I dealt with the consequences of those decisions. I used to blame the system, my father not being there or anything else to keep the pressure off myself. It was my attitude toward life. I had made so many excuses that I actually started believing that there was no way on earth that I could change because my circumstances were set in stone.

I now understand that every man I have ever known has made at least one mistake in his life. The question is, "What are you going to do to fix it?"

I wrote this book to help with my healing process and to inspire our men to stand up and claim their lives back before it's too late. We have to stop the cycle of irresponsibility and stop destroying ourselves with drugs and alcohol. No matter what, giving up is not an option. It can never be an option. We have to know that we must change and believe that we will succeed.

Do you ever wonder what you need to do when your back is against the wall? This book will give you alternatives to turning to the streets for answers.

We say, "Since my daddy wasn't there, I had to do what I had to do to take care of my family." So we sell drugs, rob and steal to keep up with the latest videos and fashions. We spend money on women we barely even know trying to impress them, but our own children don't have pampers or milk to drink. Something is wrong with this picture. I'm not knocking you for what you do to make your living, but when you are faced with the consequences of your actions, stand up. We must learn to deal with the consequences of our actions, not like boys, but as men.

No more excuses, black men. Stand up!

CHAPTER 1

Are you a Boy or a MAN?

Are you a boy or a man? This is a question that every man should ask himself. What is the difference between a real man and a boy? If you don't know the difference, boys do boyish things. Men let go of their boyish ways and take responsibility for their actions.

BOYS

Boys sit on their workable hands, but don't get jobs using them. They beg from others instead of working and getting for themselves. When the bills are due, boys look to the women in their lives to come up with the bill money, then blame her for all of his short comings. When they drop out of school, boys blame it on everything but the fact that they made a bad decision to leave school without their diploma.

When he doesn't get the job, boys blame the system and say, "The white man is holding me down." He asks for gas money from the women he is involved with because he can't afford to put gas into his own car because he doesn't have a job or he chooses to drive her car all day while she is at work. When it's time to take care of their kids, boys take the easy road out and neglect them. When child support comes after him for being a deadbeat dad, he makes more excuses about why he isn't in his child's life and how he is trying to get a job, but hasn't gone on one interview. Boys don't take care of their responsibility, but you can catch them at the club every week. Boys don't vote. They don't believe in it, but complain about who is in office. Boys don't recognize God or acknowledge him for his greatness. Instead, they worship their money and women.

He has a nice car, but he is still living in his mom's basement; girls sneaking in and out. There are a lot of boys even over the age of 30 who don't want to better themselves, are stuck in the same old job doing the same old thing and complaining everyday to the same people. When someone else gets a raise or promotion he is upset because he doesn't want others to prosper, especially before him. He could have received the same raise, but he wasn't willing to work hard for it and put in the time and effort. As a matter of fact, he hadn't been to work on time all year.

Boys refuse to be proactive. They run with their boys all day long smoking weed, and playing video games, wondering why they have straight F's on their report card or if they're older, why they have an eviction notice on their door.

I don't understand why sisters allow boys to mistreat them. They see the signs. He runs up their electricity, eats their food and mistreats their kids. He promises to get a job, but he doesn't wake up until noon everyday to begin his search.

Boys are bad examples to their kids. They believe that taking minimum wage jobs is beneath them, but have little education and no money in their pockets. Getting their own place is out of the question. They'd rather live with another female or intrude on their boys. Most boys don't even care about the women who are taking care of them, feeding and clothing them.

If she gives them money, sexes them when they want it, they think they have it made. They even brag to their friends about it. "Hey man, I drive her car all day long while she is at work and she let's me."

Boys run around with married men's wives. They can't get a woman of their own. They'd rather cheat with someone else's. Boys don't respect other people who are trying to be prosperous who may not have a lot, but are trying. Some boys sell drugs, brag about what they have and degrades everyone else who doesn't have as much money. Is that really fair to do? Some men don't have excessive amounts of money because they decided to work hard and do it the right way so boys are getting theirs, but at what cost?

Boys don't open doors for woman. They'd think they were being soft. They are also jealous of women trying to better themselves. When she gets the new job, boys pick an argument because no one is celebrating them. If she works hard to obtain her law degree, they try to belittle her or cause her to lose her self esteem. Boys don't realize that she is obtaining a higher education to be stronger for herself first and then for him.

Some boys have a lot of money. They drive nice cars and even have their own house, but can't keep the next man's name out of their mouths constantly stabbing him in the back. Their material possessions define them. They are consumed with what they have and are obsessed with obtaining more, but refuse to bless others. Boys look to people for approval instead of seeking it from God. He loves his cars more than he loves the Lord, his wife and kids.

Young boys who are bullies pick on other people in the hallways at school. Old boys who never stopped being bullies constantly pick on others at the job.

Boys never honor their elders. They disrespect them by cursing in their face, disrespecting their parents, aunts and cousins, but most of all they disrespecting themselves. To them it's cool to sag their pants and kill each other over a block that they don't even own. Boys fight without thinking, don't control their emotions and don't try to find peace in bad situations.

MEN

First and foremost, in a man's mind, God is the head of his life and men aren't afraid to let others know about it. They don't hide their feelings for the Lord, not matter who is around. All hell can be breaking loose in a man's life, but he stays focused on God and replaces his fear with faith. He knows that God can do all things and that he can do all things through Christ who strengthens him. Real men go to church to get the word of God in their spirit and live by His principles.

A man learns from his mistakes and tries to correct them. A man cries sometimes when he is hurt and isn't ashamed of it. He doesn't question his manhood. A man will work whatever job is available to take care of his family, as long as it's honest money. They pray daily and meditate on God's word, while tithing and staying involved at his church.

If he gets a woman pregnant out of wedlock he takes responsibility for being a father to his children. He doesn't need a court order to make him take care of his kids. A man listens to the woman in his life and is sensitive to her needs. Communicating with her is a priority to him.

Real men act as father figures to kids who don't belong to them. They understand that there are too many fatherless children and they step to the challenge to mentor and support other young men. When men see boys doing wrong, they stand on God's word and try to correct and encourage them to do the right thing. Men lift each other up instead of tearing each other down. When a man witnesses a boy doing boyish things, he doesn't ignore it. He tries to help the young man by leading him down the right path.

A man works hard to establish himself and attempts to work on his own flaws and his character. A man saves money for a house or car instead of trying to get them the fast way. When men make mistakes they apologize and try to make it right. They don't continue to make the same excuses. Getting themselves together is a priority.

Men lead by example. Men reach back to help other young men follow the right path and tell them of their own shortcomings to give them hope. Men understand that simply getting an education doesn't make him a man, but doing something with his education does. Real men fight their additions to drugs and alcohol, while reclaiming themselves in the process.

Real men take care for their moms and makes sure her needs are met as well, especially if she doesn't have a man in her life. They never forget where they came from. A man is proud of his manhood. He is very respectable, but firm. He learns to become flexible enough to move in and out of economic, social and political circles, all the while he doesn't pretend to be something that he's not. Real men refrain from making excuses.

The Real Men In My Life

When I was growing up, my next door neighbor's name was L.A. He was from Mississippi and played the blues almost every Saturday morning. He never attended school. He wasn't allowed to go because he grew up in the south during the 50's and 60's and had to pick cotton instead of going to class. Some of the greatest men around, never went to school, but had great wisdom. L.A. was one of those men. He knew that I didn't have a father at home, so he took me under his wings to teach me the importance of taking care of my family.

He used to let me and some of my friends from the neighborhood borrow his lawn mowers to make money. Because of him, we worked on Saturday afternoons instead of getting into trouble. We also used to borrow his bikes so we could ride around in different neighborhoods and go swimming during the long hot summer months. He charged us a small fee, but we were allowed to keep the rest of our money. He died when I was thirteen. I appreciated him for instilling in me at a young age the tools to make an honest income. He was a real man to me. He drank heavily at times, but he took care of his family. He had his shortcomings like everyone else, but fought through them. His teachings carried me into my adult hood. He influenced me to try to help out as many young men as I could.

Ralph Dowe was also one of those real men in my life. I met him when I was only six years old. Ralph was the Director of Wheeler Boys/Girls Club in Indianapolis.

He would spend countless hours there just to make sure we were on the right track. I didn't know Ralph had a family until I was grown because he spent so much time with the youth at the club. He would give us his last dime to make sure we had what we needed. He also gave the best advice and stressed working hard and the importance of going to school.

The summer before my freshman year of college, I was in football camp at Western Kentucky University when I got the call from Ralph that I had won the Indiana Boys Club State Youth of the Year Award my senior year of high school. Ralph accompanied me on my first airplane ride to attend the national ceremony in Chicago, Illinois and bought me a brand new suit to wear. I was scared to death, but Ralph encouraged me and told me I would be making many more airplane rides so I needed to get used to it. He kept me calm on the plane and helped me to feel comfortable and safe. During that trip, I had my own hotel room for the first time in my life. I was only eighteen. He trusted me and I appreciated that. I met Gale Sayers, famous Chicago Bears running back, along with other celebrities that weekend. It was memorable and even more special because I got that opportunity as a result of his involvement in my life.

Ralph always encouraged me and pushed me in everything I did. He also encouraged other young men that attended the Boys Club. He wanted all of us to go to college, preferably North Carolina A&T where he had attended. Whether we played sports or not didn't matter to him as long as we grew to become responsible men and got our education.

When he passed away in January of 2005 it was one of the saddest days of my life. He has inspired me to follow in his footsteps and work with young people to make sure they stay on track. He inspired me to teach and coach while spending less time wasting my energy on things beyond my control. RIP Ralph, you will be missed. Thanks for being an inspiration to me.

Another real man in my life was Bill White. When I was in sixth grade I met Bill's adopted son Richard at school. Richard and I became good friends and played on the football team together. One day after school I went home with him because he lived near the school and we had to stay at someone's house between football practices. It was an all white neighborhood. Richard was the first friend that I had made outside of the friends I grew up with from my neighborhood.

With time I became close to Richard's adopted parents also. When I got to high school, Richard and I grew apart, but his adopted father, Bill White, stayed in contact with me even while I was in college. I appreciated him letting me stay at his home when I was in middle school on the weekends so I could stay out of my neighborhood and out of trouble. I would stay out at their house for days at a time. He got my car fixed whenever it broke down, came to my college games and sent me $50 a month for miscellaneous items while I attended college. He pushed me to work hard in school and lifted me up when I was down. I love him for that. He truly blessed my life and always gave me good advice. He took me in, even though I wasn't his biological son.

Whenever I needed advice, he was there to give it to me. When I made mistakes he would scold me about it. Bill, or "Pops" as I would call him encouraged me to keep my grades up in school and told me to focus on my life after sports. He said that I needed to prepare myself for the next level, which I did. Everything he said was true. We are still in close contact to this day.

I met Coach Dave Enright my junior year of high school. He was our new football coach and the first to give me a chance to play after I rode the bench for seven years. Coach Enright took a liking to me from day one. He pushed me to get the best out of me. He saw something in me none of the other coaches had seen. I always knew I was talented enough to play, but the other coaches never gave me a chance.

Coach Enright not only gave me a chance to play ball on the high school level, he also pushed me to enroll in college. The other coaches told me I wasn't good enough to play on a high school level. I knew in my heart they were wrong. Thanks to Coach Enright believing in me, I got the opportunity to prove them wrong.

I had an outstanding senior year of high school and took away the Most Valuable Player honors as well. I received a full scholarship in football to Western Kentucky University. I also ran track. I went to Western Kentucky because Coach Enright had told me about Western when I was still in high school at Perry Meridian H.S. I had never heard of Western Kentucky, but I'm glad I went there. Those were the best five years of my life. I grew up during that time and received my degree in May of 1994.

Coach attended as many of my games as he could. He stayed on me to make sure I attended class and worked hard. He would even give my mom a ride to my college games when she didn't have one. He helped me purchase a car to get back and forth to school by co-signing for me. That meant a lot to me that he trusted me enough to do that. Whenever my car broke down, he would also help me with the repairs.

He is still in my life today. I thank him for everything he has done for me and for believing in me when the other coaches turned their backs. I need to point out to you brothers that this coach was not black. All white people aren't trying to take you out. This man helped me out tremendously and he didn't have to. Bill White is also a white man who helped me along the way. Both of those men took me in like family.

So I ask you again, are you a boy or a man? The definitions are very clear. It's your choice to make a change or continue to go down the same path of irresponsibility that could potentially lead to destruction. We need more boys making the jump to manhood.

Aren't you tired of doing boyish things? Isn't it time for you to step up and become a man?

Where are the men? If you're a real man, stand on it and let it be known at all times. Trust in God to lead your life instead of your education or bank account. Then after you have become a man, remember that there are other boys out there lost. They need your guidance. Give back!

Now that we know the difference between a boy and a man, it's time to work on being responsible.

Are You a Boy or a MAN?

CHAPTER 2

Being a Responsible
BLACK MAN

A Responsible Black Man

He wakes in the morning and prays not only for himself, but for his family. He understands that there will be challenges everyday so he arms himself with prayer and positive affirmations. Afterwards he gets up and gets ready to go to work so he can provide for his household. After he works a long hard day, he comes back home to his family to spend time with them, eating dinner with them if he doesn't have a night job. He spends time with his children asking them about their day and attends their sporting events and PTO meetings with their teachers. He talks to his kids about the importance of hard work and he disciplines them when he needs to, but doesn't overdue it. He is caring and loving to his wife. He treats her with the utmost respect and asks her questions about her day and well being.

He is known in the streets by his involvement in social activities that better his community and his fellow brothers around him. He attends meetings regularly and gives back to his community by working with young men and others. He attends church on Sunday, but reads scripture through the week to strengthen his knowledge of the word. He is constantly trying to get closer to God and walks away from trouble and strife.

He stays healthy by exercising, resting and eating right. He stays conscious of his health risks and takes his medication when he is faced with health problems. He doesn't eat fried foods when his doctor tells him not to. He doesn't consume himself with salt and pork when he knows it's going to damage his health. He doesn't do drugs because they will damage his mind and body and unborn children. He enjoys himself and finds time to party, vacation and just relax, but remembers to do everything in moderation.

He doesn't over consume himself with alcohol. If he drinks, it's in moderation. He fasts to spend time with the Lord.

He ends his day the same way he started it, in prayer. If he doesn't have a family, he prays for himself and his future family. He also prays for his enemies that God will change their spirit. He prays for his children even if they are not in his household and he plans his days for spending time with them. He prays for his community. He rests at night without worries because he knows that God is in control. No man is perfect, but he is who we should aspire to be like.

How do I become Responsible?

The first step to becoming responsible is recognizing both the areas in which you lack maturity and the issues from your past that are preventing you from moving forward in your life. Once you recognize your shortcomings you can start healing and getting your life on track to become responsible. Make a list of all the areas of your life that you neglect or ignore because of the pain or work necessary to turn that situation around. Then one by one, find ways to address them, whether it's not communicating with a trouble maker or finding help for your addiction.

For example, if you are a father and you are not visiting your kids on a regular basis, you are being irresponsible. Set up a schedule to see your kids. They need you. If the mom doesn't let you, go to court and fight for your visitation, but don't just sit on your hands and accept your lack of involvement because the children are suffering.

Being responsible means making an honest living and going to work. Whether you own your own business or work for someone else, responsible men find positive ways to generate revenue. Many of us may not like the jobs we have but know that we have bills and other financial obligations. A responsible man understands that until he finds a better job, any job is better than no job at all.

If you happen to live at home with your mom, there are things you can do to help her out like keeping your room clean, taking out the trash without her asking you to and helping to keep the house clean. If you are fifteen or older, you should get a job and help her with some of the bills, pay your own car payment and/or insurance. That's loads off of your parents. Don't go to the mall and spend all your money shopping. That's being irresponsible.

Spending time with God should be first and foremost. Get your spiritual life together and everything else will fall into place. Don't just spend time with God on Sundays, study through the week. Go to bible study. Share the word with your co-workers. Share the word with your family and friends.

Stay off of drugs and alcohol. When you get down and depressed pray about it. Know that it is a temporary, not permanent problem. The drugs and alcohol eventually wears off and you are still faced with the same issues. Others may turn to women or gambling and it's the same result. After that quick fix, the problem still exists. If you need help, reach out and find a program.

Join a positive organization that's trying to make a difference in your community, whether it's a fraternal organization, social club or school program helping young kids, join some effort to better your community. Don't over do it, just do your part, whether it's mentoring, coaching, etc. Our young men need your assistance.

If you are a young man, join an organization in your community or at your school. There are several organizations that promote a positive environment for young men.

When you are becoming responsible, you will realize that all of your friends will not make it along for the ride, so you will have to choose to become a leader not a follower. Some of them will make decisions to do things that are not in line with what you are trying to accomplish with your life and you have to let them go.

Responsible young men go to school everyday to get their education. They play sports or join other extra curricular activities to become well-rounded, but they realize that their education will carry them through life.

Life is all about the choices you make. I made some good ones and some that weren't so good in my past. I have the same temptations as the next man. I've wanted to buy nice things and have nice homes. I have wanted to take nice vacations and impress my significant other and take care of my family. For me and for you there is a choice to be made: "How will we accomplish my goals and desires?"

Are you willing to work hard to get what you want or will you result to doing something illegal to get ahead? Whatever you choose to do is your decision, but understand that there are consequences to your actions.

Where Bad Choices Can Lead You

Four young men robbed an NFL player's home in Miami in an attempt to steal items from his home. One or more of these young men had attended a party at the house two weeks prior. They used the party to scope out the house. They knew that most football players did not live in their homes during the football season, but this player was injured and was at home with his family.

The boys broke in to find the football player home with his fiancee and daughter. He heard a noise and went out to see what it was and one of the young men shot him in the leg. When the bullet shattered his artery, the doctors couldn't stop the bleeding and he was pronounced dead at the hospital.

The young man who killed him made the excuse that they thought he was not home when they came in to take things that didn't belong to them, and that he startled them. The four young men were very capable of working their own job to make their own money, but chose to burglarize the home and another black man lost his life in the process. A woman lost her fiancee and a daughter lost a father and none of this had to take place. Breaking into someone's house is breaking the law, whether you thought they were home or not.

Dropping out of school is a bad decision. Lack of education leads to lack of knowledge which leads to lack of encouragement and effort which leads to lack of money which leads to poverty and crime. God gave each of us gifts. Some of us have more than one. It's up to us to utilize the gifts that God blesses us with. He wants us to do all we can possibly do to make it and whatever we can't do to leave it up to him.

It's hard enough trying to find a job with an education. Most of the jobs paying good money require applicants to have a bachelor's degree or better and some won't interview you unless you meet specific educational requirements or have enough years of work experience.

I decided at a very young age that education was important. I had a vision of going to college and making it out of my neighborhood, but in the meantime, I had to survive the situation I was in. I would constantly daydream about going to college. It started when I was ten and my family was struggling. I took it upon myself to take on the role of man of the house. I guess I didn't have a choice since I was the only male in the house. I didn't have time to complain about my father not being there because my family had to eat and my mom needed help feeding five hungry growing kids and keeping the bills paid.

So I began cutting grass and carrying papers to make money. I remember us having disconnect notices on bills and making excuses wasn't going to get them paid. My mom needed my help and the only way I could help was to go out there and make some money. I thought about selling drugs to get it. It was a tempting option because the money was fast and easy, but I also thought about the consequences. I knew that doing it the right way would pay off in the future and it has.

There is nothing wrong with shoveling snow, cutting grass, raking leaves, pumping gas, working in fast food to make money. At least you are making an honest living. That's the right kind of hustle that we need to teach our young men. There is no risk or harm in this kind of hustling.

Contribute to the Household

Many young black men grew up with our moms being the head of the household. Our moms spoiled us and pampered us, so we make excuses about our lack of responsibility in our adult relationships. My mom raised me the best way she could and she did a great job, but she couldn't teach me how to be a man. I had to learn that from growing pains and from the examples of other men in my life whether good or bad.

One thing I know for sure is that there is nothing wrong with grown men being pampered by a woman, but she shouldn't have to take care of you like you are her child. Some brothers don't work, but drive her car all day and run out all of her gas and women let them do that. I don't understand how brothers do it. What are you going to do when she gets mad at you and wants you out of her house? Remember, you are not the only show in town. She's going to get tired of you eventually. Good sex only lasts for so long. It gets old. When bills start piling up on her and she realizes how much of a burden that you are and how you are not helping her to contribute to the household, all that will change. If all the bills are in her name, the house is in her name and the cars belong to her, what do you have? If you got put out today, you wouldn't have a leg to stand on.

Personally, I wanted my own stuff and I worked to get it. I like feeling the satisfaction of shopping with money I earned and knowing I've accomplished something when I purchase things I worked hard to get. I'm sure the sister in your life would rather be around a brother who is trying to make something of his life and at least holding down a job.

You can become a better provider. If you don't already have one, go out and get a job. If you dropped out, find a way to get back in school. It's not too late. No one is stopping you but you. If you are single strive to get your own car and your own place.

Just know that your starter car and place are temporary. Start out with something that you can afford that gets you from point "A" to point "B." As your income increases you can upgrade your home or car or pay your car off or get a better one.

Learning to take care of your family begins during the dating process. How you treat the women you date is a prelude to how you'll treat your wife. It's ok to date someone, but have your own home to go to. Let her breathe. Pay for her dinner from time to time and stop expecting her to always foot the bill. There is nothing wrong with a sister paying sometimes, but most of the time, the man should. You should want to pay for a nice night out. We should also teach our sons how to treat a lady. We need to teach out sons to be more responsible and to get off the couch watching Sports Center everyday and playing video games. They need to learn how to take their girlfriends out for a good time or do other things to make her feel special.

Unless you're married, you should have your own place anyway. God didn't intend for man and women to live together when they're not married. I found out the hard way, did the shacking thing before and it was a disaster because we were not married and shouldn't have ever moved in together. It needs to be done right. A healthy relationship is about giving and taking, it's not one sided. Put your money and resources together and build your empire, preferably as a married couple. Two people working together for one common goal doing it the right way will pay off.

It's a man's responsibility first and foremost to take care of his family. Some brothers go out and stay all night, partying with their boys, doing drugs, messing with different women, etc., while their family is struggling financially. How do you call yourself a man? You may want to go back and read the bible. It clearly states that the man is the head of the household, not the women. That means it's not a women's responsibility to provide for the house. She has responsibilities at the house, but when it's time to pay the mortgage or rent, that's our responsibility as men. It's our job to get out and earn money for bills, not hers.

She shouldn't have to carry that burden. If she decides to have a career, then that's great, but if she decides to stay home with the kids, that shouldn't be looked down upon. It needs to be discussed. As men the burden falls on us. That's why God made men physically stronger than women. It says in the bible, *I Peter 3:7*, that the woman is the weaker vessel. So we have to honor her work that much more.

There are too many brothers sitting at home feeling sorry for themselves, eating up all the family's food while the kids come home from school hungry with nothing to eat, running the electricity up while she is at work and playing video games is being irresponsible.

I know brothers who burn electricity, running every television in the house and blasting the stereo at the same time. It's because they are not paying the bills. If they were, they would be a little more responsible and turn some things off to minimize their cost of bills. Women shouldn't have to carry that burden. When are the men going to put their pants back on and take responsibility?

Teach Boys to become Men!

My mom was the greatest mom in the world, but she couldn't teach me how to be a man. We learn how to be men from other men. I had to learn from the streets and the few positive men I knew.

Many of us have gone through our trials and tribulations and have good jobs now, but are not giving back. If you work your job and drive past the hood everyday to get home without stopping to mentor another young man, you are part of the problem not the solution. I challenge you to mentor other young men. It doesn't cost you a dime, but you will save a life. If you have them, take your kids with you so you can teach them also. I take my son with me to as many of my speaking engagements as I can. I want him to see his dad in action so he can learn.

If every man would mentor two to three other young men, this world would be much different. Young men need someone to look up to. I challenge each of you to mentor another young man. It will do a world of wonders for your life and the young men being mentored. God took you through some things and blessed you so you could be a blessing to someone else. Are you adhering to that promise?

Don't be consumed with how much money you can make and how many people are admiring you, it's not about that. It's about what you are doing for that less fortunate brother out there who is struggling and can't catch a break. He just needs to meet with the right person to open a door for him. According to the bible, if you want to give directly to God, assist those whom are less fortunate. When you do this, you are not only blessing yourself, but you are giving directly to God.

Some black men look down on brothers who are educated. College was not talked about a lot in my neighborhood. We were just hoping to make it out of the streets alive, but you have to dream. I dreamed about going to college and made that dream a reality. Even if you grew up in a tough environment, going to school is a choice. It's cool to have street smarts, but education is the key to become upwardly mobile. There are a lot of brothers who have their education and grew up in the hood. We have to do away with the myth that being smart is not cool and being cool means that you can't be smart. Being cool is being smart. Skipping over your education isn't cool.

I remember when I was a student in sixth grade and other kids in my class would make fun of me because I knew the answers to all the questions my teacher would ask. I found myself not wanting to know the answers because of other kids teasing me until I made up in my mind that I was my own person and didn't care what people thought about me. I realized that there is nothing wrong with knowing the answers to questions. It was a good thing. There is nothing wrong with being educated, brothers, especially if you want to be able to compete with others in this competitive world.

Don't let others discourage you from learning. My education is the reason I am where I am today. When kids from my neighborhood were bussed from my inner city school to an all white suburban school, some of us took advantage of that opportunity. The students who lived near the school could either walk or drive their new sports cars to school. I felt discouraged about not having a nice car or home and often felt degraded to be going to school with so many wealthy white people, while I had to return to my house in my neighborhood everyday. But, I knew I was getting a quality education because of the types of classes that were offered to me at this predominantly white school.

After being bussed in fifth grade, all of the black students were placed in special ed classes even before we were tested. After several tests, most black students remained in remedial classes. That school system expected all of us to be dumb and many of my friends proved them to be right.

If you don't get your education, you can't blame the white man for not hiring you when the job description clearly states that you need a high school diploma or a GED. Some jobs like mine will require you to have your college degree.

Having all of your credit hours except five is not going to cut it. It's either all or none. If you didn't graduate from high school or college, get disciplined and get back in school, and get your credentials. Having your education means equipping yourself with the tools to go into a job interview prepared to properly handle the position you are seeking. This means going to class on time, picking up a book to read and not trying to make it to every party or social gathering.

I grew up with the same barriers that many of you are growing up with, but my education is the reason I'm able to do what I do, not football or other sports.

If you need help, don't be afraid to ask someone. The competition is getting stiffer and if you aren't prepared to play, you will stay on the bench. There is nothing wrong with asking for help in the subjects you are struggling with. Talk to someone about how to dress for an interview and how to answer interview questions. Everyone needs help at some time or another whether they admit it or not.

There is someone reading this right now, too proud to ask for help. They'd rather fail than to ask. This type of attitude hinders progress and success. Making it to the top is a process and we all have to ask for help at some point along the way.

A wine maker had to know the difference between making wine and making grape juice. If you crush some grapes in a short period of time, you have grape juice, but making wine takes time and a lot of work and patience. That is the kind of mindset that you need to have toward get your education.

If we don't help them the streets will!

We allow a significant amount our young men to be raised by the streets, so they turn to gangs, alcohol and drugs. We watch them as they curse in front of their elders and we stand aside and do nothing; never stepping up once to let them know that what they're doing is wrong. We need to stop acting blind and deaf when our young men make mistakes or disrespect their elders.

Our young people are disrespectful for a reason. Someone taught them to be this way. Their home situation may not be the best. Keep this in mind when speaking with them. Some of them don't respond well to authority, so be prepared for rebellion. Many adults are scared of kids, but if you truly want to make a difference, you can't be afraid. It should be the other way around. There are enough men out here to mentor these young boys.

Until we stop overlooking the problem, it will continue to exist and get worse. Don't give up if one young man doesn't respond. Keep trying. Making a difference takes time and if you touch one, you've done your job. Remember it's not going to happen over night. Most kids are used to being this way, so it's going to take time for them to change.

Young men need our encouragement and we must hold ourselves accountable to help them when they struggle. They don't know how to do certain things and neither did we. Offer to teach them how to do what is needed to be successful. Take time out to talk to a young man to see what's on his mind. Don't look down on others and remember someone helped you too.

If men would stand together, we could claim our young men back by educating them and teaching them. We have to get on their level so they will understand that we are not much different from them. These young people need to hear about our downfall and how we made it to who we are today. We didn't just get here by chance. We had to go through some things.

As the saying goes, *You have to give respect in order to receive it.* When I taught high school, I set the tone the first day of school. I let those guys know that I was in charge and they would have to abide by my rules and there were no other options, but I allowed them to voice their opinions and feelings. I also let them know that when they received their education and became the teacher or person running an area, everyone else would have to abide by their rules. We have to set the tone with our young men.

Scold them when they mess up, but show them how to fix their mistake or show them a better way for the next time they find themselves in the same situation. Lift them up when they do something positive. Explain to them the risks of turning to the streets and how it will negatively affect the outcome of their lives. Share your mistakes with them and change their lives forever.

CHAPTER 3

Learning From Our Mistakes

We all have made our share of mistakes. I know I have. Mistakes helped to groom me into the person I am today. Growing up in my neighborhood was tough at times, especially having no brothers and no father to look to for guidance. Everyday I left the house could potentially be fatal for me and I knew that and dealt with that fear on a daily basis. I can relate to young men going through this right now.

I felt like I really needed guidance and felt lost at times without it. Some people don't understand the impact that a real brother can have on your life. There was only so much mom could do for me and she did a lot, but when I left out of that house, I was on my own. Many of the skills I picked up were learned in the streets from friends and watching others in my neighborhood. Me and my boys would sit around and listen to the older guys talk about women and other things and would try to pick up advice that we could use later.

We thought we were cool when we mocked the older guys. Some of my childhood friends were Poncho, Petey, Willie "Cornbread" Anderson, Big Ben Thompson, Larry Shotwell, Tony Binion, Herb Dove and Isaac Booth. My boy Tony was killed when I was sixteen years old. He was only fifteen. He was shot at a party. It scarred me for life, because he was just an innocent bystander in the wrong place at the wrong time. He was the first of my friends to die.

My buddy Larry was also killed when I was in my mid-twenties. He was murdered and they never found his killer(s). Both of their deaths still hurt to this day.

I think about them quite often. We used to run together as kids, trading clothes, trading stories and playing sports together. We always tried to stay up with the latest fashions, even though we didn't have a lot of money. My friend Tony had my sweatshirt and I had his jacket, which I took with me to Western Kentucky when I left for college. I held on to it all through college before giving it away to my roommate to try to get past his death because I never really moved on. I had nightmares all the time. I wondered how I could have prevented their deaths and why they died so young.

We all knew what was going on around us, but we stayed involved in sports and tried to stay out of trouble, but sometimes trouble still found us. You can walk a straight line all the way through life and be in the wrong place at the wrong time and trouble will find you.

Trapped by Material Possessions

I learned that making mistakes teaches different lessons. Some of the lessons learned are painful. Many of us are where we are today because of mistakes we've made. I had many friends that sold drugs. We were poor and drugs brought in a lot of money.

I know plenty of guys murdered because of selling drugs, so the money isn't doing them any good now. The money doesn't do you any good when the judge gives you fifty years. I know guys serving thirty and forty years fed time in prison where they have to do 95% of their sentence. Two of my students were killed out there selling drugs. They were only twenty-one and twenty-two.

At one time in my life I wanted to sell drugs. I was tired of being without and not having enough money to pay bills. I was tired of seeing my friends with the nice cars and a pocket full of money. I felt like the drug dealers had it going on. It seemed that they had all the women, all the jewelry and all the money. I would see their motorcycles and get fascinated. I always wanted a motorcycle like that. Well I have one now, but got it through hard work.

Their clothes were not like the clothes I had on. The women they dated looked like models and worshiped them, while my boys and I were struggling just to get a date. If a new pair of shoes came out, they had them first and I wanted those shoes too. They had the drop top old school cars with the shining rims and candy paint and I was impressed by that when I was younger. We were in the hood and couldn't believe that they could actually afford that stuff.

I didn't had a car with rims on them with a booming system or a car at all at that time. I remember at that time LL Cool J had a song called, "Boomin System" and it was playing in just about every car and truck in my neighborhood. These guys didn't seem to have a worry in the world. They would go to the mall and just spend like it was nothing and I didn't have any money. They ate at places I wanted to eat at. They would ride through the hood and pull over while their fans ran over each other to get to them to see their new ride.

That made selling drugs even more tempting, especially since my pockets were empty and I was walking instead of riding. People asked me all the time, "Why didn't you do it? What kept you from selling drugs and following in their footsteps? Everything you needed to get started was right there in front of you." They were right and I was recruited by all the drug dealers in the neighborhood. Everything was right there, but I chose not to be like everybody else. I didn't have the best clothes, but I had a piece of mind. I didn't worry about someone robbing me because I didn't have anything. I was confident in who I was even though I wasn't gaining attention from all the ladies at the time. I wanted material things just as bad as everyone else, but I decided to wait until I could afford them.

I witnessed first hand how drugs tear down neighborhoods and families. I witnessed friends killing friends and family members turning on each other. I witnessed black on black crime and it was all over money and drugs. I just couldn't bring myself to do it. I was my own man. I said to myself, "If you can't get it working and doing it the right way, God doesn't want me to have it." My closest friends wouldn't let me do it either.

Most of the drug dealers I knew were killed by someone close to them who got jealous of their success. I watched how family members and friends would fight over their possessions. Even the drug dealers that went to prison were betrayed by close friends or family members as well. Their own friends turned them in to the police. I thought about my future and I could envision how selling drugs would eventually destroy my life and impact other lives around me, like my family or my friends.

If you are selling drugs, brothers, just know that there is a price to pay. You will pay it now or later, but you will pay. I have not met too many brothers who retired from selling drugs. There was a big drug bust over in my old neighborhood some years ago and I knew all the guys in it. The police took everything, leaving nothing for their girlfriends, wives and kids. They even took the dogs. It was all on the news. It was like a dream or something. I couldn't believe it. These were the very guys that everyone wanted to be like. Each of them received sentences of twelve to thirty-two years of fed time. All of their possessions were auctioned off. Everything was left in the midst of their days like the bible says in *Jeremiah 17:11*. All the fun was over. Now they are making forty cents a day behind bars. It was good when it was good, but when they got caught, it came to an abrupt end.

If I gain nice possessions, I would like to be around to enjoy them. I'm not knocking anyone for selling drugs, I'm just asking you to think about what you are doing and the impact that it could have on you and your family down the line.

Remember that there are consequences for your actions, brothers. I know a lot of brothers that died rich. The bible explains what happens to you when you get money the wrong way. I have never met anyone who took it with them. Why spend your life in prison when you have the tools that God gave you to get a job. Why spend an eternity in hell over stuff that never belonged to you in the first place.

Those same skills can be used to do something positive. Start your own business and live a normal life. You can get rich by working, if you work hard and smart. What good is it to get rich and lose your soul in the process?

Sometimes we are given second chances to learn from our mistakes, but we refuse to move on. Brothers go to jail for selling cocaine, do their time and then come back out of jail just to pick up where they left off. We have to learn from our mistakes and move on. Taking the same risks will produce the same results: frustration and loss of freedom and rights. Your mistakes are character builders, but you will not continue to get chances to get it right. Choose to take a stand, change and leave it behind you. Be your own person. If we don't correct our mistakes, we will keep passing them down to our sons and daughters and their sons and daughters.

Some of my friends decided to walk away from dealing and work and they didn't make a lot of money right away, but they are married with kids now and are doing well financially. It's a tough life to live. Does this happen to everyone? No, but most of the guys I know either ended up dead or in prison. Our young men have the same mentality me and my boys had when we were younger get rich quick. They want the fast money, the bling bling and nice cars right now. They don't understand that making money and being successful is a process.

It's like learning how to walk as a baby. You crawl for a while, then you take baby steps and stumble for a while, then you learn to walk and get stronger doing it every day. You go to school, get your education, work hard day and night and pursue the career of your choice.

Consequence of Disobedience

The bible says to honor your mother and father. One day, I decided to do my own thing and disobey my mother and it almost cost me my life. She had warned me about going across 30th street to go to the store because she knew that it was very dangerous for me because of some of the rival gang members. I really wanted this certain kind of candy, so I thought I would be able to sneak across 30th street to go to the store and get back without my mom knowing.

The store was only two blocks from my house, so I thought, "What could go wrong?" When I crossed 30th street, I had only walked a half a block before three boys jumped me from out of no where. I was only eleven years old at the time. Two of the boys were bigger than me and one of the boys was younger. The big boys grabbed me and held my arms behind my back. The smaller one came up to punch me in my face. They wanted my shoes and my fat lace shoe strings. Fat laces were popular in my neighborhood back in the 80's because of the rap group, "The Fat Boys."

I decided to play tough guy that day. I told them they weren't getting anything from me and attempted to break loose. One of the big boys pulled out a Rambo knife and pressed it up against my throat. It was big and sharp. I felt like my life was about to end. My heart was beating out of control. He pressed the knife against my neck so hard that it began to cut my skin and bled a little from the pressure of the sharp knife. The three boys began to drag me behind a house to finish me off when an older man yelled out of no where and told them to leave me alone and they ran off.

I was thankful that he saw me, because I may not be here today telling this story all because I disobeyed my mother's orders. I truly learned from that mistake.

If you are a minor you are supposed to obey your parents at all times. My life was almost cut short because I decided not to.

I only remembered one of the boys from that incident. I remembered him because he was a little meaner than the other two. He was a big bully who had gone to jail several times for robbery and had served time in prison for killing a pizza delivery man who was delivering to his house. He received a twenty-five year sentence for that crime.

He had served eleven years before his release. What he did to me never left me. In fact, I often had nightmares about it for years. Can you imagine being pulled behind a house to your death over a pair of shoes or fat shoe laces? One afternoon, I had a taste for some Popeye's® Chicken, so I decided to take the trip to 38th and Keystone in Indianapolis. After I ordered my food, I stepped back to wait on my order. When I turned around, I saw the same guy who had pressed the knife against my throat and had attempted to rob me when I was a kid. He still looked the same. My heart was beating fast, but not out of fright this time. It was out of anger. When I saw him, my appetite left me. I wanted to get even with him. All of that built up anger in me came back and consumed me as I approached him. I remembered how he had scarred me that day and all the nightmares I had experienced through the years.

I didn't even think about it. This guy had almost taken my life and I wanted him to pay for it. I wanted him to experience what I had experienced after that incident. I wanted to take him out right there in the restaurant, but I had a few questions I wanted him to answer first. I asked him, "Do you remember who I am?" He looked at me strangely then said, "No."

I walked up closer to him and repeated the question to him. I had flashes of his knife against my throat. I was now a 22 year-old young man going into my senior year of college. I asked him a third time, "So you don't remember me?"

He started looking at me strange and I saw the fear on his face as he slowly backed up. I said, "Why are you looking so scared? Don't you like picking on kids?"

By that time he recognized me and his hands began to shake. I wasn't that frail little frightened eleven-year old kid he had attempted to rob twelve years prior. I was a 5'11, 225 pound football player with a loaded nine millimeter in the back of my pants and one of those bullets had his name on it.

He didn't have a crew with him this time. He was all alone. Most cowards get scared when they don't have an audience with them to cheer them on. I reminded him of how we knew each other and he looked as if he lost his appetite also. As he backed out of the door I followed him outside. I pulled out my gun and pointed it at him. He took off running like his life depended on it out in the middle of traffic on 38th Street, one of the busiest streets in the city. He ran frantically, weaving in and out of traffic. I wanted to pull the trigger. The devil kept telling me to pull the trigger, but God showed his grace. One side of me wanted to shoot him, while the other side said, let it go. I thought about my family and how upset they would be. I thought about how hard I had worked to get into college and I was going into my last year before graduation. I also had pro scouts from the NFL coming to my practices and games. As he weaved in and out of traffic, I put my gun down and walked away. I praised God that night for giving me self-control to not pull the trigger.

Not too long after that, the same guy was murdered execution style. The murderers tied his hands behind his back and shot and killed him at close rang in front of his kids. To date, they never found the killers.

We have to make the right decisions because split second set-backs can destroy our lives. Some of you have been faced with far worse circumstances than the ones I described. I pray that you make the right decisions.

Bad Decisions

That summer proved to be a trying one for me. A couple of months before I was to report back to school for football camp, my sister's boyfriend asked me if he could take my car to the carwash. I thought it was weird of him to ask me if he could wash my car, but I knew he was trying to get in good with me since he was dating my sister. He had asked me to hang out with him a few times before and I turned him down. I didn't make a habit of hanging out with my sister's boyfriends just in case they broke up or stepped out of line with my sister, it would be easier for me to handle.

One day he asked me if he could take my car and wash it. I was hesitant at first, but then I thought, my car needs to be washed so why not. About an hour later, he came back to my house acting weird so I immediately knew something had happened. I asked him what was wrong. He just stood there. I walked out to my car to find out it had been wrecked. I asked him what happened to my car. He told me that after he had washed it, he backed up with the door open to the vacuum and the door got caught onto the cement block that held the vacuum cleaner.

He apologized and said he would fix it before I left for school. I reminded him I had to leave early for school because I had football practice and camp started before students came back to school. If I was going to go pro in football, this was the year I needed to perform.

Time had gone by and it was getting close to where I had to leave for college. It was three weeks to be exact and he hadn't said anything about when he was going to fix my car. I was driving a beige 84 Cavalier. I loved that car because it was reliable and had never gone down on me since I bought it my freshman year of college.

Two more weeks had passed and my car wasn't close to being fixed. I was due to report to camp in one week and I was growing impatient, so I decided to pay him a visit. I knew where he worked, so I went to his job. My buddy gave me a ride to the supermarket. I walked in the door and my sister's boyfriend was working as a cashier. I politely walked up and asked him, "When are you going to fix my car. You promised to fix it and I have to leave for college next week for football practice and I won't be back for a while."

It's tough to get home during the season and I didn't want to ride around my senior year with a messed up door on a beige car. He brushed me off. I asked him again about my car. He said, "Fuck you and your car."

Everything that happened after that was a blur. I do remember snatching him over the counter and beating him in his face. Two of his co-workers grabbed me and he tried to run. I shoved his co-workers down and ran outside after him. I know he didn't think he was going to get away. Didn't he know I ran track? I caught him in the parking lot and threw him into the side of a car that was driving past and punched him in the face again. His manager ran outside to protect him. Reality sunk in and I realized what kind of mistake I had just made. I was about to panic. There were hidden cameras all over the place.

I lost it when he had cursed at me about my car and blew me off. The last thing I wanted was to go to jail and miss my senior year of college for doing something stupid. My buddy and I ran and jumped in his car, but it didn't start right away. We both panicked and jumped out and began running down the street. Then we realized that we weren't going to get very far, so we ran back to the car and it started this time. My friend did 80 miles per hour getting out of that parking lot.

The police came to my mom's house later looking for me, but my mom said she hadn't seen me. The next day, my sister's boyfriend called my mom crying, telling her what happened. After a few days had gone by, my sister encouraged her boyfriend to drop the charges as long as I promised not to beat him up again. My sister put a door on my car, but it wasn't the right color. I thought, "It's better than nothing." I got teased on campus, but my car was still running and my friends still asked me for rides.

I couldn't believe that I had made such a dumb decision that could have cost me my education, my career or my life.

I decided to be grateful that I didn't go to jail or worse and left the situation alone thanking God that I made it out without seriously injuring him or worse. I left for camp on time and had a great senior year. I also graduated from college on time and went to the NFL as planned. I could have continued to pursue her boyfriend and really gotten myself into trouble, but I learned that day that it wasn't worth being sought after by the police.

My next lesson took place with another one of my sister's boyfriends. This occurred a year after I had graduated from college. My sister had gotten into an altercation with her live in boyfriend and he had physically assaulted her and my nephew. I was used to them getting into fights because it took place quite often, but this particular time he had been drinking and I had somehow become his target. He called my house after my sister threatened to call me about him messing with her. He was cursing at me telling me that I was scared of him.

I was already on edge about my mom being hospitalized with kidney problems. I hated it when my mom was in the hospital. It drained me, because she would be in so much pain and I felt hopeless in my ability to help her. I told him not to call my house again and I hung up the phone. He called right back and began calling me names, telling me he just hit my nephew and I was next.

I let my temper get the best of me that night. I felt like this guy was testing my manhood calling my house like that. My first thought was *I can't let him dis - respect my house or me.* If I did, *He might as well move in and take over.* I felt that if I didn't take a stance he would have thought I was soft and continue to come after me.

I jumped off of my couch and put on some jeans and tennis shoes. I also grabbed my nine millimeter and stuck it in the back of my pants as I drove to his house. When I got to the door, he opened it and pointed his gun to my head and threatened to shoot me. I should have known that he was talking a little bit too strong and should have figured he had a gun or something on him. As he held the gun to my head, my life flashed in front of me. If he pulled the trigger, I knew

I was dead and at that time, I really didn't care. I had just gotten cut from the Minnesota Vikings, my mom was in the hospital, my best friend had just gotten murdered and my girlfriend and I were on the verge of breaking up.

I found myself not caring about anything at that moment. I felt that I had reached my limit and wasn't about to take anything else off of anyone. I told him to pull the trigger. He just stood there.

I said it again, "Pull the trigger."

He said, "Don't temp me," as he moved closer to my head with the gun. Although it was an accident, he had already murdered someone and did jail time for it.

I told him if he was any kind of man, he would put the gun down and fight me like a man. I guess he gave my words some thought, because he put his gun down.

I reached in my pants to grab my gun and I put it down. We began to fight. He only got in one punch before I started hitting him with some head shots and body blows. I gave him a hard one to his side and I could see the pain in his face. He said, "That's enough, I quit." He was in obvious pain from the hard shot to his ribs I gave him. Holding his ribs, he ran and picked up a nearby chair and proceeded to tame me like I was a lion, trying to keep me off of him as I moved forward calling him a coward. I asked him, "What happened to the tough guy that called my house threatening to take me out? He's no where to be found." I attempted to get past the chair and hit him again, but he took off running to the back of his house. He went to retrieve his pit bull to make him bite me.

As he brought his pit bull to the front of the house where I was, I picked up my nine millimeter and cocked it back to get it ready in case his dog tried to attack me. As soon as I picked up my gun, I heard sirens like the police were near by.

I didn't know at the time, but while we were fighting, my mom called the police from her hospital bed. She knew I was over there and we were probably fighting or worse. She also knew that I had a hot temper. After I heard the sirens, I threw my gun into a nearby field next to the house. My sister's boyfriend followed suit by throwing his gun in the field also.

When the police arrived, they asked what was going on and we both said nothing was going on. He told both of us to go home or go to jail. I didn't waste any time when I got the green light to get in my truck and I quickly drove off. I came back later that night to grab my weapon. I didn't want any kids to find it the next day and play with it.

This was another case where, not only did I dodge going jail, I dodged death. God was not ready for me yet. He was preparing me for a much greater calling of ministering to young men. My sister's boyfriend could have easily killed me that night or I could have killed him. He apologized several times over the years. I told him, "Let's put it behind us and move on."

We get along well now. God is amazing. Many of our young men don't get that second chance to reconcile. I learned from that mistake and never went back over there or to anyone else's house in anger with a gun tucked in my pants. I learned that my sister and her boyfriend's dysfunction was none of my business and I should have ignored his calls. The outcome could have been different.

Run-in with the Law

Years had gone by and I had kept my nose clean. I thought for sure I had made it this time. I was finally growing up. At least I thought I was. I was on my way to Michigan, driving from Indianapolis, to visit a female friend I had met in Miami a few months prior. It was a sunny beautiful afternoon. The traffic wasn't too bad for a Friday evening and I was bumping my 2Pac CD as I rolled down the highway. A few hours into my trip, the sun began to go down and I knew it would be dark soon. I was half way there when I noticed that someone kept flashing their lights behind me, blinding my sight in my rearview mirror.

A big truck behind me on huge wheels flashed me several times blinding me. I couldn't see anything. The driver also honked his horn at me profusely. I quickly changed lanes, but the truck followed me everywhere I went. We went back and forth for a few minutes and then the truck changed lanes and began to roll up next to me slowly rolling his window down. I was in my Expedition, but the truck still towered over me because of the larger than normal wheels.

In my neighborhood, when someone rolls up on you rolling the window down slowly it was usually a drive by shooting. I didn't want to take that chance, so I reached under my seat and grabbed my nine millimeter, pointed it in the direction of the truck and fired it as it rolled closer to me. I aimed slightly above it though. I only fired one shot before the truck backed off as it weaved and almost ran off the road.

My heart was pounding. I knew I didn't hit anyone in the truck because I didn't shoot directly at them, but I shouldn't have fired that shot until I found out what was going on, but I didn't know if it was safe to wait and find out. I wanted to let them know that I wasn't going quietly if they were going to shoot me.

I continued my journey up the highway, when I noticed a car following me once again. This time it wasn't the big truck. It was a police car. I could see the lights even though they were not on yet. At first it was one police car, then within minutes it was two, then five, then eight and finally it was so many that I couldn't count them anymore. I quickly called my boy Bill in Detroit to tell him what was going on since I was half way to Michigan. He was in shock. We talked a few minutes about what had happened and then all of a sudden I could see police lights flashing for days behind me. I couldn't believe so many police cars were back there. It had to be at least twelve to fifteen of them. I just knew I was going to jail. Bill agreed, but stayed on the line with me in case he needed to come and bail me out of jail. I was in the middle of no where, so I could only imagine what jail in a small town would have been like. I didn't see a brother in sight either.

It wasn't long before they pulled me over. I had on a white tank top and a long pair of Air Jordan shorts and white Air Force One tennis shoes. It was the heat of the summer. The police told me to show them my hands after I finally pulled over. I thought about how easily I could be mistaken for grabbing something, so I quickly put my hands out the window and as much of my arms as I could. I didn't want any surprises.

I had never had this type of encounter with the law. All of them had their guns pointed at me. I just knew it was over for me. I said to myself, "One of these cops is going to shoot me and claim it was an accident or self-defense." I said, "I'm going to jail." Neither sounded promising to me.

When I got out of the car and they noticed my size, it made things even worse. I put my hands up above my head to show I didn't have any weapons. Out of the fifteen or so police officers on the scene, one in particular kept trying to provoke me to get smart with him. He called me boy several times and made other disrespectful comments. He came close to me and asked, "Do you have something that you want to say to me boy?" I didn't reply at first then I said, "I don't see no boy around here." I knew he was waiting on me to do something or make a false move so he could have a reason to take me in.

Another officer took my license and registration. Then two of the officers began to check my truck with their flash lights. Then one cop got into my truck and looked up under the seat where my nine millimeter was. He grabbed it and said, "It's still hot sir," to another officer. The policeman took my gun back to his swat car. I was thinking to myself, "You are never going to see that female you were on your way to see and you are going to be in jail for a long time."

I remembered what had happened to Michael Taylor when both of us were sixteen years old. Michael was in the back seat of a police car with shorts and a tank-top shirt on and somehow the police claimed that he shot himself in the head while he was handcuffed in the back seat of the car. Where he got the gun from, no one knew. It still remains a mystery to this day and I didn't want a similar situation. I felt like my heart was going to jump out of my chest.

I stood there on the side of the highway with fifteen or more white police officers awaiting my fate. An officer approached me, while the others stood close by. I assumed he was coming to cuff me, but he asked for my gun permit instead. I had it in my wallet and proceeded to get it when the same cop who had been bothering me earlier had come back.

He said he would get it for me. He grabbed my gun permit and gave it to the officer. I wasn't sure if my license was valid in Michigan so I prepared for the worse. I knew I had crossed the state lines about 30 minutes prior to being pulled over. The officers kept me on the side of the road over an hour. Cars were riding pass slowly to get a good picture of what was going on. One person yelled "Rodney King" out his window as he drove past.

I assumed that my license and license plates were being run to find out if I were a criminal or something. They were also deciding if they were going to take me to jail or not. The officer asked me, "Did you shoot at someone not too long ago?"

I explained what happened with the big truck flashing their lights on me and told them that it scared me so I flashed my gun at them to scare them off. I never admitted to pulling the trigger. I knew I would be gone for sure if I did that.

Another officer asked, "Why is your gun so hot?" I told him that I had gone to the firing range prior to making my trip to Michigan as I was praying to God at the same time to forgive me for lying. I still thank him today for sparing me. If you don't believe that there is power in prayer, you're mistaken.

The police kept my gun, but let me go. I pinched myself several times to make sure it was real. *Let me get this right, you have a black man on the side of the highway with fifteen white police officers with guns pointed at him and he walks away with no bruises, gun shot wounds or jail time?* Yes, that was God intervention and I gave him all the honor and glory. I went on to see my friend that weekend, but didn't forget what happened. It took me some time to swallow it.

I told this story because many of us have made similar mistakes or even worse, but God has spared us with another chance. Not only do we need to learn from those mistakes, we must also bless someone else with our story in hopes that it will detour them from trouble.

That was the last time I had shot at someone. Brothers learn from your mistakes so you don't repeat them, but use your stories to minister to others. These young men need to hear about our pitfalls and bad decisions. They need to know that we have made mistakes, but learned from them. Don't look down on these young brothers today out here messing up. Most of them are misguided with no direction and it's up to us to help them turn it around.

CHAPTER 4

Discipline

Anything you do in life requires some form of discipline. You need discipline while you are in school, work or just hanging out with friends. You can't attend every party or function in college or you will flunk out. Ask someone who has done this in the past. When you graduate from college and get your own apartment, it takes discipline to keep the rent and other bills paid on time. If you have to choose between paying your bills and partying for the weekend in Miami, discipline should encourage you to pay your bills. Whatever profession you decide to go into will require some discipline, whether it's working at a fast food restaurant, working in a corporate setting or working your own business.

Discipline can be taught. Many of us are not born with it, but learn from our parents, coaches or teachers. It goes beyond hard work. Sometimes it's making the right decision or having the right people around you. Other times its saying no to your friends who want you to do drugs for the first time.

Len Bias, star basketball player from the University of Maryland, was drafted #1 overall by the Boston Celtics in 1986. His friend talked him into trying cocaine for the first time and it proved to be a bad decision. After sniffing cocaine, it burst his heart and he was pronounced dead when the paramedics came to pick him up. All of his hopes and dreams were ended because of one bad decision. All the hard work he put in the gym was for nothing. That's how quick it can go wrong.

Discipline stops you from doing something you know you may live to regret the rest of your life. Discipline stops you from trying drugs for the first time when you know that your uncle is strung out. Discipline gets you out of bed when you know you need to be at work or you will be fired. Discipline makes you come home at night when you've been out with your friends hanging and clubbing. Discipline sends you home to your wife instead of to some other woman's bed who means you and your family no good. Lack of discipline has wrecked hopes and dreams.

I learned discipline at a young age from my mom, who was the man and woman of our house. She did not hold back when my sisters and I messed up. Her discipline was swift and sometimes hard. Discipline is having the will to do the right thing, even when you are under pressure. When my mom said to do something, you did it, no matter what it was. If you didn't do it, you knew you had consequences to deal with. My mom did not hesitate to grab the belt or switch or whatever else she could find to get you in line. My sisters and I felt her wrath on more than one occasion. According to the bible, in *Proverbs 13:24, He who spares the rod hates his son, but he who love him is careful to discipline him.* My mom lived by this rule daily.

I know I deserved most of my punishments. I was hard headed at times and thought I knew everything, but her discipline carried me through high school, college and my professional life. I was raised the old school way. When I was a kid, the principal or Dean would paddle students when they got out of line.

At times, my neighbors would discipline us too and then tell our mom when she got home from work so she could get us again. I still believe in this type of discipline and feel that our young men are lacking it. The rules have changed. Kids can call Child Protection if they are hit by their parents. Kids need that kind of discipline. I wouldn't be where I am today if my mom hadn't disciplined me the way that she did. It carried me through high school and college. When I was faced with certain situations that I knew were not good for me, I could hear my mom's voice even though she wasn't there. When I was at a party, I could hear her saying, "Don't set that drink down and walk away." It made me think twice.

Besides paddling, my old teachers from grade school would pull out their ruler and ask unruly students to hold their hand out to strike them with it. I can still remember being paddled and hit with a ruler by my old teachers. I'm a grown man now, but it has stuck with me all this time. After teaching at Arlington High School in Indianapolis I realized that our kids are lacking discipline because teachers are not allowed to discipline them like our old teacher's disciplined us. Instead, they fear their students.

Teaching Discipline

There are many ways to teach discipline. It doesn't always have to be done with belts or rulers or paddles. I learned a lot from playing sports from the time I played little league up to the pros. In my professional life, I still live by the same principles I learned in sports.

Besides sports, discipline can be learned from playing chess, participating on a debating team or playing in the band. It's important for parents to find out what their children like and get them involved ASAP. Don't let them just sit in the house all day playing video games. My mom kept me involved in extra-curricular activities daily, like the boys club or basketball, which helped deter me from trouble when it came my way. I was too busy to hang out.

I believe that being in sports and other activities saved my life, but it wasn't an easy ride. I wasn't naturally gifted like many athletes I knew growing up. I had to out work everyone in order to succeed. I wasn't very strong or fast when I first started playing sports. It seemed like the other boys were five steps ahead of me in skill level. I knew that I wanted to compete though, so I made up my mind to out work my opponents. When we ran sprints, I tried to run harder and longer than anyone else. When we hit the weights, I went that extra mile.

My cousin Gary, a natural born athlete in football, basketball, wrestling and anything else he got involved in, was extremely strong on the weights, so he taught me the ropes. When I first started working out I was one of the weakest, but before I graduated from high school and college I was the strongest. I was also one of four of the fastest guys at my high school and on my college teams.

I put in a lot of hard work and it took discipline and sacrifice. It's not easy getting on the school bus by yourself when its summertime and all of your friends are playing ball outside. The school bus would take the inner city kids to our high school, 45 minutes away from our homes, to lift weights. I had to make a choice to either play with my friends or ride the bus to get into shape by myself. I took many journeys on that bus by myself in the summer and when each school year began my teammates wondered why I was so strong. I was accused of using steroids and everything else. I took several drug tests and passed them all because it wasn't drugs, it was discipline and hard work.

You don't have to be like some of these pro ball players who cheat by using HGH steroids. Just work as hard as you can and do the best you can. Have the discipline to get up in the morning or late in the evening to run and lift. Do more than your opponents are doing.

Tiger Woods and Michael Jordan are both champions in their perspective sports, but people have no idea of the hard work, preparation, countless hours, and discipline it took to make them the champions that they are. They are number one and if you listen to both of them, they are mentally and physically tough which takes discipline.

Some of my high school teammates didn't want to acknowledge the fact that I was working out hard and improving my skills everyday. I guess they would have known that if they would have worked out hard instead of being lazy. Sometimes I was the only person on that activity bus going to school to lift weights. They would have been stronger and faster just by working harder.

I remember how slow I was in track in middle school. I was the only young black kid running the 1600 meter run (mile) instead of sprints like the rest of the black males I competed with and against. I ran that mile pretty good though and it prepared me to become a better sprinter, but it took discipline for me to change events. It wasn't an easy transition. I knew how fast the sprinters were that I was competing against. I continued to stay focused and worked on my speed often.

My test finally came, but I was prepared. I had worked out for two years on my own to prepare me for it. When I lined up to race those upper classmen to challenge them for a spot on the varsity 4x100 relay team and 100 meter dash, I was confident. I made the varsity track team as a sprinter that year as a sophomore. I beat out several upper classmen. The following year our relay team was sectional and regional champs and we went to the state finals. My senior year was a repeat of my junior year by winning a Sectional and Regional Championship and going back to the state finals.

Sports not only instilled discipline in me, it also taught me the importance of being a team player, the importance of being on time. I still remember consequences of being late to football meetings.

Consequences of being Late

I had gone to Florida to celebrate spring break with some of my college teammates. My college coach at Western Kentucky University was Jack Harbaugh, a no nonsense coach who was known for kicking the best players off the team because they either challenged him in practice or weren't attending classes on a regular basis. He had previously warned us to be at the team meeting on time. He wanted to make sure everyone got back to school safely and on time. Coach was not apposed to making his players run for being late. His hard lesson of being on time spread quickly through our locker room. He didn't have much remorse either. My teammates and I felt like the coaches enjoyed making us run but I believe he was really teaching us to be more disciplined about being on time.

My friends and I had a great time in Daytona Beach, Florida with my freshman roommate, Melvin Johnson, who was from there. We hung out with Melvin all week, partying, hanging on the beach and talking to girls from other schools. It was my first time to Florida and it was the best spring break I had ever experienced.

After a fun week, it was time to head back school, so we loaded the car, timed our trip and got on the road. I already knew we had a team meeting that night, but we left in plenty of time with time to spare so I felt that we were cool. The trip was going pretty good until the traffic on the highway came to a halt. Traffic was backed up for miles and we couldn't figure out what was going on.

We finally received our answer to why the traffic was backed up. We were caught in an avalanche. Large rocks had fallen on the highway so traffic was slowing up to get around the big boulders. When we finally got through traffic we were at least two hours off schedule to make it back to school on time for our team meeting. There was nothing we could do about it. Even if we went 100 miles an hour we were going to be late and all of us knew it.

Even though we made it through traffic safely, coach would not understand why we were late. I felt sick to my stomach. I thought about the horror stories of others who had already experienced being late in the past. One of my teammates said he ran so much that his legs were sore for a month. I could only imagine what my punishment would be.

I wanted to blame it on the natural disaster but who would believe us? I thought, *I left on time so how did this happen to us?* Excuses are excuses.

When I arrived late, coach was extremely upset with me. The meeting was to ensure everyone made it back on time and I missed it. I was still young, but a leader on the team and it didn't look good that I was coming back late. Coach Harbaugh only said four words to me, "See you Saturday morning." I already knew what I had in store, but once I got there, it was even more than I imagined.

My teammates and I arrived Saturday morning around 5a.m. as instructed. This would be a morning that we would never forget. Our coaches ran us to death. We ran stadium stairs, did push ups, rolled all the way down the entire length of the football field more than once, did sit-ups, more running, lap after lap after lap. I thought it would never end. The sun was beaming down without a cloud in the sky. It was so hot out there, it felt like we were in Las Vegas in the heat of the day in the middle of the summer. It's get extremely hot in Vegas in the middle of the summer. As the morning went on it became hotter and hotter.

One of my teammates passed out on the field but no one cared. He was told to get up and finish. We felt sorry for him, so we helped him up and encouraged him to finish, but we could barely keep up ourselves. It seemed like the day would never end. My legs felt numb. My whole body ached. The coaches ran us until they got tired of watching. The punishment lasted for over three hours that morning and I have never forgotten it. We were barely allowed a water break. It was the most severe punishment I had ever experienced in sports.

I was never late to another meeting. In fact, I used to show up to meetings first. I would set my clock when I took a nap and was paranoid, checking it every 5 minutes to make sure it was working and I didn't oversleep. That experience taught me the importance of time management and better planning. Maybe I should have left a day early or a few hours earlier to give myself more time.

This is the type of discipline our young men are lacking. Going to school is a joke for most of them. They don't believe in being on time. Whether it's going to class, going to work or just paying bills, being on time is extremely important and could be costly for those who don't adhere to it. Being on time was a pet peeve of mine as a teacher and a manager. I became very upset when my students or employees were late.

Demanding Respect

When I taught I had severe consequences for coming to my classes late. Young men who came in late were subject to do push ups and sit ups for their tardiness. When a young person used profanity in my classroom, there were consequences for that as well. Teachers need to be tougher on these kids and our judicial system should back them. Classrooms should be run by teachers, not students. I remember walking past classrooms to see kids sleeping or cursing at their teachers. This behavior was unheard of when I was a child in school. I got paddled again on one occasion because I turned and looked at the teacher who paddled me and she thought I gave her a dirty look.

We need some strong teachers who are not afraid to take their classrooms back because too many kids are taking over. If you don't believe me, walk through the halls of a high school in the inner city where you live. There is no telling what you are going to see. You would be amazed. The rules have changed so much.

Teachers don't possess power in today's school districts. Instead, students can curse, spit at them and even try to fight them without serious punishment. That's why these students are so bold. Teachers should be able to teach without being disrupted by students who probably shouldn't be there in the first place. If a student approaches a teacher in a threatening manner, teachers should be able to defend themselves without consequence.

My buddy, Onaje Pinkney, who taught at Arlington High School with me, wasn't intimidated either. We held each other accountable for the mission we were trying to accomplish, which was saving our young black men by any means. Onaje and I shared similar backgrounds. We were both former collegiate athletes who cared about the plight of our young black men so much that we took jobs in teaching. We were those two teachers in the building that none of the students wanted to mess with because we weren't afraid of fighting back.

This unruly behavior starts at home where children call their own mothers bitches or worse. In a lot of homes, kids are practically raising themselves because their parents are either out working or out partying and drinking. Whatever the case may have been, I didn't play that mess and attempted to teach discipline to every young man I came into contact with.

My motto was, "If you run up and put your hands on me, that means you want to have a date with the floor or concrete." Young men were thinking because Onaje and I had our education that we were two soft guys and would-n't defend ourselves. We were just two black male high school teachers who cared. Onaje and I didn't accept disrespect from kids and teachers today need not accept that behavior either.

Kids were scared of us and we weren't out there to scare the kids, but we wanted to instill some discipline in them. We wanted them to be respectable men and learn the importance of controlling their emotions. We wanted to remind them that teachers are the ones who went to college and received their teaching degrees and therefore earned the right to be respected and to run their classrooms the way they saw fit without unnecessary disruption.

You can't change the world, but if you can touch one child then you have made a difference and done your part. I lost a few here and there, but for the most part, most of the young men knew I cared about them and they respected me for what I was trying to do. Even when I see them today ten years later, they still show respect.

He Picked the Wrong Day

Some found out the hard way that I meant business. I had a student who stood six feet and weighed about 220 pounds. He was often disruptive in my classroom. He would make loud outbursts and used profanity in every other word that came out of his mouth. I would put him out on occasion for his profanity. One day, the student decided that he wanted to take it to the next level and put his hands on me. Big mistake! Since he was bigger than the other kids, other students were intimidated by him. I played football with and against guys twice his size and was not impressed with his size.

I told him to leave my class for his behavior and on his way out the door he brushed up against me real hard to make some physical contact. I didn't react to that so he got bold and reached out and grabbed my arm. I couldn't believe he decided to put his hands on me, but I acted quickly to set an example for the whole class to see. My students witnessed him bumping me and were equally shocked by his actions. I asked him to leave my classroom and he said, "Make me."

I tried to call down to the office, but before I knew it, he had put his hand on my arm again. I quickly grabbed him and slammed him to the floor face first. I put my elbow in the back of his neck while his face was smashed into the floor. I whispered in his ear saying, "Don't ever put your hands on me again or you will pay dearly." I didn't want that to happen, but teachers can't go around letting people treat them that way. After his several attempts to break free were unsuccessful he just laid there. Every time he tried to move, I would put more pressure on the back of his neck. He could have hurt me or someone else and that's what our teachers face on a daily basis and it's unfair. Our young men are lacking discipline and respect.

As I let him up the police were there to apprehend him. It's tough dealing with an undisciplined young men who constantly disrespect their own mothers. Our teachers should not have to deal with this nonsense day in and day out.

News traveled fast through the school about the incident. He was supposed to be the toughest guy in the school and I was told by other students, that he had mentioned to others that I was his target. I hope he got what he came for. From that day forth, I never had trouble with him. I spoke to my class that day and let it be known to every student I had encountered that if they decided to do what he did, the results would be the same if not worse.

Every young man needs to step into a teacher's shoes. Teachers are important people in our society and should be looked upon and treated as such. There are a few teachers out there who are not fair to students and don't care about our young people learning, but a majority of our teachers do care. Students should not have the opportunity to disrespect them. If they do, they should pay for it.

Our school systems are in need of strong black male teachers to interact with younger black men and teach them the discipline they desperately need.

Stay on Course

I didn't disrespect my teachers, but my attitude wasn't right. I remember being kicked out of school on several occasions for fighting or having an attitude. Ralph Dowe, former Director of Wheelers Boys Club, once said to me. A man who lacks discipline, lacks character and direction.

How many times have you heard a story of a brother who was supposed to go pro in football or graduate with honors from college, but ended up in prison or strung out on drugs? I can name plenty of them who fit the description. When you go down the wrong path knowing it's the wrong path, you're asking for trouble.

One guy from my neighborhood was the first black superstar that came out of our high school. I looked up to him when I was in middle school. He went to high school with my oldest sister. He was 6"1," 215 pounds of muscle and very popular at school with all of the teachers and students.

He was also the first black male to win Homecoming King at our predominantly white school. Everyone had high hopes for him. Because his grades weren't so great he ended up going to a Junior College, but was later picked up by Division I-AA Illinois State University. He was roommates with a friend of mine.

His first year at Illinois State was like a dream come true. He performed very well and was already hearing talk from scouts about going to the NFL. Because he went to junior college, he only had two years of eligibility left. Everyone was projecting him to go pro the following year.

During the summer after his first season at Illinois State, he didn't work out and wasn't as hungry to succeed as he was his first year there. He didn't work out as hard as he did his first year. In fact, he reported to camp, noticeably out of shape and over weight. It didn't help that he didn't pass his running test.

Every college football player has to take a running test when he comes back from summer break. This is the coaches way of finding out if the athlete actually worked out that summer. Based on his performances his coaches could look at him and tell he was definitely out of shape.

Nonetheless he was still given the starting nod at running back because of the job he had done the previous year. After four games into his senior year, the coach decided to start a freshman running back in front of him. From what I'm told, his teammates teased him in practice because he lost his starting job to a freshman. He blew up at his coach at his final homecoming game of his college career because of his lack of playing time. Many of his family members attended the game and he wanted to put on a show for the home crowd. He let his frustration get the best of him. The coach benched him and told him to get off the field and go to the stands with his family and friends so that's what he did.

He was benched for the rest of the season, disappointing his family and friends. Throughout the year when he left the football field he was down after most games because he didn't get to play. Other young football players started to lose respect for him. Needless to say, the NFL wasn't knocking at his door like everyone expected.

Everything else is speculation, but shortly after he graduated from college he was gunned down just a block away from his house. There were rumors that he had gotten into the drug game, but it was never verified. I just remember my mom calling me back home to attend his funeral during my sophomore year of college. I was in shock and couldn't believe what happened. His death affected me and made me paranoid every time I came home to visit my family during our breaks. I had followed in his footsteps and went after all of his records in high school. His death was tough on me and other young upcoming football players in my neighborhood. I really had to check myself and refocus.

I learned that you can do the right thing, go to college, play sports, obtain your degree only to lose focus and come home and get involved with the wrong people and get killed.

No Practice, No Play

So many young black men are wasting their talents in and out of school even though they don't have to work as hard to be successful as those who came before them. Playing outside like we did as kids has been replaced with video games. Kids are overweight because of lack of physical activity. After coaching high school track, I realized how lazy our young people really are. We practiced everyday, but only a select few would come.

Most of the guys would quit because they didn't want to go through the tough workouts that were designed to make them champions. They wanted to just show up on meet day and it didn't work that way. I didn't allow that as a coach. No practice, no play. I warned them that the lazy work ethic on the track would translate into their everyday lives. After talking to some of those former student athletes, they proved it to be true. Many of them quit everything they started and most of them are still trying to find themselves.

Several of the other youth that I have taught in the past are now adults and understand how important it is to have discipline. They have their own homes now. They are paying their own bills. Some of them are married.

As parents, we hinder our kids from succeeding by not letting them grow up and make mistakes. As parents we have to be disciplined enough to teach our children and then let them learn the consequences of lack of discipline so they won't make the same mistakes over and over.

If you tell them not to spend over a certain amount and they decide to exceed that amount, they need to be responsible for the overage. Don't send them extra money. They have to learn discipline when it comes to their money and how they spend it. Our children have to get used to falling back on their own two feet, not ours. When we allow them to, they grow and appreciate things more. When they spend their own money, they learn the importance of the dollar. We must require them to work around the house or in a real job for the extra expenses they want to incur. When they work for the things they want to buy, they appreciate them more. Even if you can afford to have your kids stay at home and not work, they should experience and be taught the importance of earning their own money. They will appreciate it more and will be prepared for the reality that you will not always be there to take care of them.

As men we have to strive for discipline in order to stop making the same bad decisions. Young men are looking up to us and what they see is what they will be. Let's lead by example and teach them the techniques of discipline as we continue to grow.

CHAPTER 5

Get a Job!

In order to eat, pay your mortgage or rent and take care of your responsibilities, you will need money. That means you will have to work, or risk doing something illegal to make money. If you would like to stay out of jail, get a job.

Real men take care of their families and responsibilities. Some men work day and night if they have to in order to take care of their families. If you don't have a job, don't blame the white man and society for your unemployment issues. Whether someone caused you to lose your job or not, excuses won't get you another one. Put those excuses behind you, move forward and focus on your next move. It's going to take hard work and preparation to find a new job.

You can't get a job sitting on your couch drinking beer and flipping channels with the remote. Employers need to know you exist and that you are available. Applying for jobs is simple nowadays. All you have to do is sit in front of your computer and send your resume to any employer in the country or abroad. If you don't want to leave the house you don't have to. Otherwise you may want to consider attending job fairs or hitting the pavement to fill out applications onsite. You can't get a job if you never try.

Shortly before my son was born, I wanted to save money so in addition to teaching and coaching, I did personal training some evenings and I worked at night as a bouncer some nights until 3:00 a.m. I'd get up the next morning to start over again. I was tired, but I did what I had to do to take care of my son.

When you aren't bringing in anything, working a minimum wage job is a better option than no option at all. How can a person make fun of people working at a grocery store when they're walking around with lint in their pocket? I was talking to this brother the other day and he was telling me how the white man is trying to stop brothers from making money. I guess he wanted my sympathy, but I had to speak some truth to him. He was right, some white men don't want us to make any money, but the last time I checked, I controlled my own decisions and choices.

I choose to take advantage of the opportunities that have been afforded to me. Even though our country is sometimes prejudice and I know that sometimes I will have to work five times harder than the next man, the opportunities are still there. We have to stop getting discouraged and turn that negative energy into a positive job search. Anything you decide to do in life that is worthwhile is going to take hard work and sacrifice.

In one of my previous jobs as a Lead Program Manager for a housing agency, I was burned out on what I was doing. I was tired of not making enough money and tired of working around people who wasted a lot of valuable work time. I enjoyed my job, but was ready for a change. I had goals I wanted to reach in the near future and wanted to put myself in a position to get there. Instead of fussing and feeling sorry for myself, I started my job search. I knew I wanted to be in pharmaceutical sales, so I researched and found out as much as I could about that field of work. I read books, studied interview questions, looked on the internet and researched to see what I could find. I had several friends in the business who were very successful, so I leaned on them for their expertise. One of my friends in the business came to the rescue and helped me prepare for my interview. I knew other reps from other companies also. I would pick their brains for good information I could apply to my job search. I pulled all of my resources together and prepared for the next step in the process, the interview.

I studied the websites of several different companies, researching their products, mission statements, benefits packages, territories, etc. I tried to find anything that would be helpful to me during my interview. Even though I didn't have one scheduled yet, I knew an opportunity was coming. I believe that positive thoughts bring positive results. I went online to find out what kind of interview questions I might be asked so I could get a head start. I applied the information I gathered from all those sources. I made every effort to become prepared. I wasn't going to rest until I got the kind of job I wanted.

If you walk into an interview thinking that you won't get the job, then you probably won't get it. Remain positive because hard work pays off. That's the attitude you have to have when going after the job/career you want. It's not going to be easy and no one said it would be. Just getting in front of potential employers to showcase your skills can be challenging. The hurdles, like posting your resume and doing a phone screen prior to a face to face can sometime take extra work and effort.

Steps to a Successful Job Search

1. Start your search via the boards: internet, job fairs, networking, etc.

2. When you begin interviewing, don't give up when doors are slammed in your face. The right job for you will come your way.

3. Find resources that will assist you in your job search.

4. Don't be afraid to seek help from those who have been successful in the business.

5. Study sample interview questions so you know what to say when you are faced with challenging questions.

6. Ask well thought out questions during the interview.

7. Dress for success. Make sure you are well groomed.

8. Arrive fifteen minutes ahead of schedule.

9. After your interview, ask for the interviewer's contact information. Follow up by sending a thank you e-mail or note in the mail.

A More Professional Appearance!

I was advised by an older gentleman, Ray Satterfield, who told me that if I planned to climb the corporate ladder I would have to make a change to my image and my attitude. He told me that I was very smart but hot-headed and that my temper was going to get the best of me if I didn't get it under control. He encouraged me to cut my hair and change my dress code.

As a result of his honest advice, I stopped wearing jeans to work and replaced them with slacks and suits with collared shirts and it changed the way people looked at me.

I cut my hair to have a cleaner look for the opportunities I wanted to pursue in the present and future. I had freedom to wear my hair like I wanted, but decided that if I wanted to move up the ladder, I needed to change my image. All this was done by choice, my choice. As a result I felt more respected and people took me more seriously. I'm not saying you are headed down the wrong path because your hair is braided, but I don't know too many CEO's of companies with corn rolls not, including Sean Carter (Jay Z).

If you plan to move up in the corporate world or society you will have to sacrifice some of your ways and adjust your appearance. Unless you aspire to be an entertainer, wearing braids will get you overlooked on most levels. Sagging your pants will get you passed over as well. I'm not suggesting you not exercise your right for individual expression. There are many cool brothers with clean hair cuts and well groomed faces. You don't have to sacrifice who you are, just how you dress and the things that come out of your mouth when you're in the work environment. In fact, I like the changes I've made. It has opened more doors for me and it has allowed me to open more doors for others.

It's a process and processes don't occur overnight. Don't get discouraged. It took me time. I was a college graduate, working a good job, but I still wore braids, twist or an afro. I was young and rebellious. I wanted to do things my way and my way worked for me while I was younger, but as I got older it changed. I followed the advice that Ray gave me. Shortly thereafter I was promoted to Lead Program Manager overseeing my whole department.

Moving up in the corporate world requires you to fit the part and it's hard to fit the part when you come into an office with your own style, trying to do things your way. Fitting the part means being professional whether it's in the way you dress or your communication style. If you're communicating with your supervi-

Getting Ready For Your Interview

1. **Dressing for Success**. Sometimes you may not have dress clothes to wear to an interview. Just dress neatly in what you have. Put your shirt in your pants, pull your pants up to your waist and wear a belt. Wear dress socks with your shoes.

2. **Wear dark colors**. You are not going to a celebrity event or club, so leave the loud colored clothes at home. Wear dark colors like blue, black or brown for your interview.

3. **If you have a suit, wear it**. If you don't have a suit, purchase a new one or used one at a thrift store, borrow one or connect with your local community service providers like fraternities, 100 Black Men, etc., to have one donated to you.

4. **Come well groomed**. Cut your hair if it needs to be cut and shave your face and trim up your mustache and beard to have a neat look. Take a shower and put on some deodorant. Don't put on too much cologne. It's not cool to do that. Even though you may think it smells good, you're going to run everyone out of the place.

5. **Ask for Help**. Contact another man in your local area for suggestions if you don't know how to dress or watch some of the business men around you to get ideas. Find out where suits are being given away in your neighborhood or contact your counselor or advisor to ask for suggestions.

sor the same way you communicate with your boys, you're probably not being professional. We tend to be a little more laid back around our friends.

What you decide to do on your own time is your business. I love old school hip hop and grew up listening to it. I can't really get into some of this new rap. I'm not understanding it, but too each his own. When I'm not working, I'm in my Yankee fitted hat low to my head and Sean John Jeans or Roca Wear Jeans and a shirt. That's my time away from work. Other times when I hang out with my friends, I don't wear a suit. I dress in comfortable jeans, hard shoes and a collared shirt. I ran into one of my customers one weekend and he didn't know who I was because of the way I was dressed, but on Monday morning, I was back in my suit. Even rappers dress up on occasion. Flip your style sometimes. It's okay.

I have taught classes in the past instructing young men how to dress neatly for interviews, including teaching them how to tie a tie. I even let them keep the ties they practiced with. I have not always had my choice of clothes to wear to interviews, but I wore what I had and made it as neat as possible. When I'm interviewing a young person, I look at their appearance. I don't care if they have a suit or not. I just look to see if they are making the most with what they have to wear by being neat and well-groomed.

After You Get the Job

If you're persistent, you will get a job. Once you are employed, don't forget what you committed to do in the interview, like working hard, being on time, not getting into any trouble. Do not cut corners at your job because someone is always watching and taking notes and will use it against you later. Get to work on time. Do not be late every day and have an attitude when someone says something to you about it.

Just because you have the job doesn't mean haters won't be lurking, looking for a reason to get you fixed. Even after I got my ideal job, trouble still came my way. There are haters everywhere you go, even when you are one of the top sales reps in the country like I was with my former employer. Some people dig ditches and wait patiently for you to fall in like giving you bad advice hoping you will use it, causing you to get fired or lying on you to your boss or teammates to paint a negative image of you. Because I serve a God who can make a way out of no way I believe that whatever he has for you is for you. If you are having trouble on the job, fight it but don't lose your cool and don't complain every time someone hates on you. That's why we call them haters, because they hate on others. Don't go down without a fight. Read your employee handbook to get options to fight your case.

Surviving the Workplace

1. Stop blaming the white man for your troubles and your mistakes even if he is trying to cause problems for you, especially in the work place. Individuals within the system will make it hard for you sometimes, but many times you make it hard on yourself. So take responsibility for your own actions and focus on what you can control.

2. Document things you are leery about and keep an accurate record of things you don't agree with. If you have attempted to remedy the situation make sure you have the dates, time and course of action you used. It will be helpful if you have to fight for your case.

3. Understand that everyone isn't out to destroy you. If you believe that your co-workers are your enemies, it can cause you to treat them unfairly.

4. Stay away from negative people who gossip on the job or constantly complain. Their negative vibe could easily rub off on you and cause you to lose focus on the positive aspects of your job.

Fighting Racism on the Job

Yes, black men have been harassed and discriminated against by racist people in the workplace, in subtle ways, but we have to find ways to fight back without losing our tempers and going to jail. It's tough being a minority in the corporate world today because it seems that you are expected to work three times as hard as your co-workers and most times make less money with more responsibility. You are expected to react and when you don't react with hostility and they call you an angry black man. Racist people search deep to try and find other ways to get under your skin or to try and tarnish your credibility.

When you stop feeding into their schemes, you are fighting because you are using discipline and focusing on your purpose, not your co-workers. You keep your nose clean by ignoring those kind of people. When someone tries to start something to get a rise out of you, stay focused on where you are trying to go and don't throw it away over their negative behavior. They can't win unless you let them. Too many of us are giving up too soon right in the middle of the fight. If you are being treated in a way that is unprofessional, fight for your rights and ride it out to the end. Take it to your union or get you an attorney, but don't give up. It's not going to be easy, so you must have some endurance.

I know a brother who had a promising career with a big company. He was on his way up the ladder, but couldn't get his attitude together. When people made little comments to him, he would, react to their statements before thinking and appear unprofessional and out of control. He began yelling at one of his co-workers for cracking a joke about him.

Eventually it was used against him when he was up for a promotion. He was told that he couldn't manage people because he couldn't handle adversity amongst his peers and had no control of his emotions. As a result, he lost his focus and a promising job.

As brothers we have to be willing to fight for our rights. You have a right to be the CEO of a Fortune 500 company. If you have put in long hours of hard work, don't throw it away over unresolved anger. Our ancestors were treated a lot worse than us. We look at some of the most successful minorities in the business and we have no idea what they had to put up with to get there. Remember how Jackie Robinson broke the color barriers in baseball; a black man playing on an all white team in an all white league in 1947 during the height of the civil rights movement. He went to work everyday under distress, but never quit his job. He paved the way so other minorities would get the chance to play major league baseball.

Remember, there is going to be struggles, unfair treatment and sometimes discrimination in the workplace, but you can't get short-sided. Know what your individual goals are and don't let anyone deter you from them. Focus your attitude on those goals. Don't allow the obstacles that you will likely face stop you from reaching your goals.

Fighting for Your Rights on the Job

1. Let your haters hate and move on. Don't allow their negative energy to affect your work.

2. Follow policy at all times even when others don't.

3. Read your employee handbook and find out what your rights are.

4. Make sure you are responsible, like getting to work on time. Do not take extended lunch breaks and don't lie about your hours worked.

5. Be a leader at your job whenever possible, but understand that sometimes you have to be a follower to be a good leader.

6. Do your job to the best of your ability whether someone is watching or not because hard work pays off.

If you lose one job, go get another one

Things are going to happen. On the job there's always the possibility of getting laid off, having your shift changed or getting let go because of poor performance. Your manager may be hard to get along with. Be flexible and mindful of your surroundings. Give God the victory even before your situation is worked out and don't let others bring you down. Challenge your manager when you are being treated unjustly. Don't let them just fire you if you didn't do anything wrong. Seek legal counsel before you walk away. Then turn it over to God and trust in him with all your heart and lean not to your own understanding.

If you are forced to walk away, understand that you are not tied to a job or a supervisor. I remember a preacher stating that we don't have jobs, we have assignments. Your biggest assignment is to serve God. Jobs come and jobs go. You can always get another job. So, don't think it's the end of the world because you lost yours. It's just the beginning for a new opportunity. Keep your cool at all times not matter what the situation. Vent when you get home, not at work. Get focused and prepare to conduct a new job search while you're working on your case. Be patient and use this as an opportunity to explore your options.

When you are going after a job of any kind, there is always competition. Think of what you will do to separate yourself from the rest of the pack. What positive attributes can you bring to the table? How and what will you do to go that extra mile? Employers look for this quality and you have to be smart about it. If you can, speak with someone who works at the company you are considering to find out about their policies and procedures and what they are looking for. Find out as much as you can about the manager or supervisor, including the management style and the kind of person they are looking to hire. It's tough finding top talent these days and companies are becoming more strategic and competitive in the way they hire new people.

Have some confidence when you go into interviews. You must believe that no one is better suited for the open position than you. Carry that attitude with you both during and after the interview. It must be embedded in your brain. Although people in your life may not believe in you, it's very important that you believe in yourself. If you have not convinced yourself that you are supposed to be there, how will you convince the person interviewing you?

Waiting on someone to find a job for you will only hinder your search. It's time to live up to your potential. If you don't like your job or the money you are making, begin your steps to finding a new one. If you get fired, don't complain; fix the situation by finding another job. If you want a better position, it never hurts to get more training. Take a course or go back to school. No matter the case, be sure that you do everything in your power to get a job.

CHAPTER 6

Why You Being a Hater?

What is the definition of hating? Where did it come from? When did it start? Some would say it started when the serpent started hating on Adam and Eve after God blessed them to eat whatever they wanted except for the forbidden fruit in the Garden of Eden. God blessed them with everything, but the serpent tempted them to eat the forbidden fruit. That's a player hating move. He wanted them to self-destruct after God had blessed them. The serpent couldn't stand seeing Adam and Eve happy.

Others would say that it began when Cain started hating on Able. His younger brother was being blessed by the Lord and he didn't like that. Cain was tired of hearing how great Abel was so he put a stop to it. He killed his own brother in a jealous rage.

Maybe it began when we were slaves. We were robbed of our name, robbed of our language and our minds. Slave owners stole us from our country and later would pen one muscular brother against the next to see who would win the fight. Brothers were hating on each other because they were made to in those days. Nowadays white men don't have to instigate. We do it to ourselves.

You should never be jealous of another person, no matter what, because God has enough blessings for everyone. He did create the earth and everything on it. I love to see others prosper and doing well, but brothers hate on each other everyday. If you don't believe me, look at the news. You will hear about a brother killing or harming another brother like it's nothing.

Haters come in all forms and sizes and have different titles. They hate on you for no apparent reason at all. I'm used to be hated on. It used to bother me, but I had to realize that haters don't control my destiny. I used to wonder why people hated on me, but now I could care less. I'm a Christian and will continue to strive to be the best I can be but everyone makes mistakes. Some people judge you off your mistakes, but God is your judge, not others.

If you call yourself a man and you have a problem with another man, why can't you just go and tell him instead of talking behind his back? Personally if I have something to say to you, I'm going to bring it to you. As men, we should be able to come to each other when we have a problem and talk it out instead of back stabbing and fighting or shooting each other. We have already been through too much together as a race of people.

In the 70's the Black Panther Party was broken up by haters. There were people inside the group giving information to the FBI and others causing the Black Panther Party to be destroyed. One of the founders of this prestigious group ended up strung out on drugs while others went to prison. The group was taken down little by little until all of them were wiped out. This group of brothers and sisters stood up for equal rights in the mid-1960s into the 1970s but lost it's power because of haters.

Don't waste your time worrying about people hating on you. They are only doing their job. Hating is what they do, so let them do it. Don't expend energy on something you can't control.

Brothers killing brothers for no reason usually goes back to hating. One brother is making more money than the other or one brother has a fine sister with him and the other doesn't. There are men in jail or dead right now as a result of haters. Why is that? Guys are snitching on each other, getting jealous of each other, trying to have what the next man has instead of getting their own. It's sad to see brothers taking each other out.

Stop Hating, Start Doing

When I was in middle school, with no physique and no chest, I was talked about because I didn't have a nice body. When I started running and working out in the gym and became more muscular in high school, I was talked about because other brothers couldn't lift as much as I could or didn't have a physique like mine. I was hated on either way.

Other times I was accused of using drugs. I was the strongest on my team and worked hard to earn that title. I didn't need drugs, but guys who weren't as strong as I was tried to make the excuse that I was juicing to handle the self-doubt they had about themselves. I don't even know what steroids look like and I have never used them, but they were going to hate on me regardless. That's what haters do.

A person can't go into the weight room and play around for ten minutes and leave expecting to be able to bench press 425 pounds. It took hard work and determination for me to get there. My attitude was, "No pain, no gain. You have to sweat tears in the gym."

It's so funny to me how guys really want to be someone other then themselves so they talk about the person they wished they were to make themselves feel better and to cover up for their shortcomings. Jealousy, envy and hate are destroying our society. I never understood why brothers chose to succumb to such a negative way of reacting to one another. If you want muscles, lift weights. If you want a flat stomach, run, do cardio and stay away from the Twinkies^{TM} and Cheetos^{TM}. Don't hate on me because I was disciplined enough to do it the right way. Don't hate on LL Cool J because he's 40 looking like he's 30 because he's in good shape. Get off the bench and get in the game.

Haters have all the tools, they just refuse to use them because they are too busy looking at what the next man is doing. There are enough boats to go around. There are enough mansions to go around. There are enough cars and diamonds for everyone. There is enough money to go around for everyone, so work for it and stop focusing on other people's stuff. You don't have to hate on another brother because he got the position. There are plenty of positions out there for everyone. You may have to expand your job search, go with a different company or relocate, but there's no reason to hate on him for getting the job. The show doesn't stop because one person got the promotion. There are plenty of promotions to go around waiting for you to grab one. Again the opportunity may be elsewhere. Seeing other's being successful should motivate you to do the same.

It excites me to see another brother doing well. I have several friends who own their own businesses, houses and properties and I'm happy for them because I know they worked hard for their success. I have friends who are

CEOs over big companies and I'm happy for them also. No one knows what they went through to get to where they are today. Their accomplishments encourage me to work harder for my own and to model myself after their achievements. Others have played professional sports or enjoy a lavish life as a result of their job in sales.

A few years ago I couldn't even get my hair cut because of my former barber gossiping about me. We were supposed to be friends. We traveled and went in and out of town together, but he couldn't seem to keep my name out of his mouth. I remember when I got cut from the Minnesota Vikings of the NFL and my barber was cracking jokes about it. That was one of the toughest days of my short life, but he thought it was funny. He fed off of my pain. Every time I turned around someone else was asking me why I still hung with this guy because he always had something negative to say about me. But he always wanted to be around me. I never understood that part.

I guess he wanted to be around me so he could continue to find things to hate on me about. He fed off other brothers' hurts. If someone was going through a tough time, he celebrated it. When someone lost a girlfriend or a wife because of making a mistake, he made sure that everyone knew about it. How can you feed off another brothers pain and suffering? If you feel stronger when others are hurt, something is wrong with you. If you feel joy in your heart when someone else is suffering, something is wrong with you.

I had to remove myself from him because I can't be around people who are jealous of me. If you are around guys right now that are jealous of you, who talk about you all the time–it's no secret who they are –recognize it and cut them off.

Haters are all over. Some of them are your friends, others are your teammates, while others you don't even know. Again, they are only doing their job. Hating is what they do, so let them do it. Don't expend energy on something you can't control.

Hating on Your own Brothers

You hear about young people killing each other all the time because of material things. When haters see a young brother walking down the street with waves and the girls are checking him out, they sit back in a jealous rage. Get your own waves. Go get you some wave grease and a brush and tie your scarf around your head at night before you go to bed. Stop trying to be like someone else.

Young brothers see another brother wearing Sean John or Roca Wear and want to rob him instead of working hard and getting their own. What's stopping them from getting a job and buying their own gear? When haters see another brother moving up in the company, instead of celebrating his success, they envy him and become jealous.

When I worked for the Housing Agency, I moved up through the company pretty quick. I had my share of haters in my previous position, but most of it came from my former manager. She didn't want to see me prosper. She was so busy dumping her work on me, that she didn't know she was building me up to be the man I am today. She taught me everything I knew by dumping her work on me and I thank her for that. I worked hard under her, but she was never happy with my performance. I was under constant criticism. She even took credit for some of my work. I was doing her job, but not getting compensated for it. She thought she was getting over on me, but God used her as my footstool because she lost her job and I was promoted to her position making more money than she was making. I was also the youngest manager there at the time.

Hating on each other is a tragedy. If you are a hater, stop! Work with what you have and who you are and stop worrying about getting what the next man has. It's enough stuff for everyone to enjoy. God has blessed all of us in different ways. Some of us don't have because we don't ask. Some of us don't have because we can't even be faithful with what God has already given to us.

Hating on the Man of God

Why do people hate on pastors? They are planting churches, not dope houses. They are building young men into leaders and strong fathers, not tearing them down. Not only are they saving souls but they are also feeding the hungry, clothing the poor, providing jobs and training for the unemployed and providing scholarships for students and adults seeking higher learning.

Don't worry about what these brothers have or what they did in the past. Have you ever sinned? God forgives us of our sins and they are not God, they are preachers. No one is sweating the lawyers and doctors about what they have. You decided to do what you do and they decided to preach the word of God.

My pastor doesn't drive a big Benz like some other big name pastors, but if he did, why would someone have a problem with it? He deserves to drive a Benz. He works for God. Some people don't want to see the pastor prosper. They'd rather see drug dealers driving a Benz than the pastor. Drug dealers ride up and down the street in nice vehicles and nothing is said about it. In fact, people often praise them and try to get close to them to get a piece of what they have. They can pull out a bank roll and nothing is said about it. If a preacher pulls out a bank roll, everybody starts gossiping.

Preachers are regular people like you and me. They have to eat, clothe their children and provide for their families just like you do. If a preacher builds his congregation from twelve people to 12,000, shouldn't he get a raise? If you build your business from twelve employees to 12,000, don't you deserve a raise or should you be paid the same salary you received when you only have twelve employees?

There are people worrying about the money they put in church and where it is going? The bible says in *Malachi 3:10*, bring the whole tithe into the storehouse. If you don't bring the tithe to the storehouse, you are doomed. Some people hating on the preacher have never brought their ten percent to the church, but complain. Don't get me wrong, if someone is ripping you off, then you need to say something, but when you pay your tithes at church, you are not supposed to worry about where it goes because it's in God's hands and it's his money anyway. If you die tonight, your money is not going with you.

Shouldn't your pastor receive a fair salary for his work? If the preacher is not handling the other money properly, that's between the preacher and God. Furthermore, align yourself with a church and pastor who allots money for programs, gives back to the community and works to upkeep and/or improve the worship facility to bring in more members and services. Get involved in the ministry if you would like to make a change..

Why do haters want their preachers to live poor and drive a beat up car and live in a run down house? You don't want to live poor and drive a beat up car, so what makes you different from the pastor? Haters want to take their kids out to eat and on vacation. What makes you think the pastor doesn't want those things for his family? Why do you hate on the preacher when he comes into church clean? You like nice suits don't you? I know I do. Preachers like a lot of the same things that you do.

When a preacher's kids get sick, he has to take them to the doctor's office, just like you do and it cost money. When his car breaks down, he has to take it to the dealership to get it fixed and it cost money. If he is a false prophet, God will deal with him in his own way, so don't judge.

Shake those Haters Off

When I decided to work in pharmaceuticals, I had haters on my team. I knew that I would have to work extra hard to get the job, but I didn't know I had to work as hard to keep the job. I was ranked #1 in my region and the top five percent of the nation and two of my team members hated on me daily. I was blowing out my numbers and goals, but they would constantly find faults in everything I did. They would go into offices and paint me as an overly aggressive person to my customers in hopes that it would deter them from doing business with me and would often have private team meetings without me being present.

I made more on one bonus check then the both of them combined over a two year period. Haters are everywhere. They try to dig ditches for you, but God is in control. He will use your haters to elevate you, like he did for me. I left that company and joined another one by using the great numbers I made at the first. I have the same territory that I had with the first job. Now they have to watch me prosper even more because I'm calling on the same docs with a different company. If God has it for me, it's for me.

If you aspire to be something great but your boys are telling you that you can't make it, don't believe them. Believe in yourself. Stay focused and go after your dreams.

Negative friends are toxic to your success. Some of your biggest haters are the people closest to you. They stay close to you so they can find out all of your business and then when you get into an argument with them, they throw all of your faults back in your face. They bring up all of your business that you buried in your past. It's sad that you can't really trust some people. I have been burned by people close to me more than by strangers.

Surround yourself with positive Christian men. If someone is constantly negative and it bothers you, you need to remove yourself. Evaluate who your true friends are. You find out by seeing how they react when you are down. When you go through your lowest points pay attention to who inspires you in a positive way versus who puts you down and who makes you feel worse.

If you are the one doing all of the hating, check yourself. Hating should be a crime. If I were the judge, I would give out citations to haters and charge them like they were speeding. You will never prosper if you keep putting the next man down.

CHAPTER 7

Fight the Powers that Be

Flavor Flav and Chuck D of Public Enemy said, "Fight the Powers. You have to fight the Powers that be!" How do we fight the powers that be?

Fighting Our Fathers' Absence

Statistics show that 66 percent of black children grow up in single parent homes where the father is not present. I have to agree with Roland S. Martin who wrote in a *CNN.com* commentary, "Black Men Must Reclaim Our Children."

The decaying value of life in the inner cities clearly can be traced to the exodus of fathers from the lives of so many young men. Excuses often are tossed about as to why black men leave their children (and their children's moms) to fend for themselves. But a lot of them are just sorry and refuse to accept the responsibility that comes from raising a child.

...But if the person who impregnated that woman were on the scene, not only helping to pay for the raising of the child, but also serving as a strong influence, I just don't believe we would see such a chronic condition.

I was one of those kids. In fact, I never met my biological father. He never came around for my first step, my first touchdown or my college graduation. Like many other irresponsible men out there, he impregnated my mother and walked out of our lives leaving me out in the world to fend for myself. I didn't see a picture of him until I was 30 years old. By then he was already dead. This cycle is very common in our society. Young black men all over the US are born every-day and taken care of by their mothers, born and then forgotten by the men who made the choice to leave, running the streets like we never existed.

I was one of those kids. In fact, I never met my biological father. He never came around for my first step, my first touchdown or my college graduation. Like many other irresponsible men out there, he impregnated my mother and walked out of our lives leaving me out in the world to fend for myself. I didn't see a pic-ture of him until I was 30 years old. By then he was already dead. This cycle is very common in our society. Young black men all over the US are born everyday

Coping with a Father's Absence:

1. Understand that his leaving had everything to do with his own insecurities and lack of responsibility and noth-ing to do with you so don't blame yourself.

2. Accept that you can't change the past, but remember that you can make better choices when you have your own family.

3. Forgive your father for leaving you. Release the anger that you feel toward him. (Very hard to do, but neces-sary for your healing).

4. Find a mentor or join a positive group. Join a club, church group or youth group to be around other posi-tive men and learn how to occupy yourself with positive activities.

5. Love yourself no matter what. God made you, so you are somebody special and no one can take that from you. You need to recognize that at all times.

and taken care of by their mothers, born and then forgotten by the men who made the choice to leave, running the streets like we never existed.

I must admit that today at times it still bothers me that I never knew him, but I made up in my mind that it's time to stand up and face the music. My father walked out on me, but that doesn't mean my life is over, that I should keep making excuses about my actions, blaming it on him not being there. I was angry at him for a long time. And it wasn't until I forgave him that I was able to get a handle on my emotions and the way I viewed myself.

I remember fighting in the streets and getting in trouble. Boys would pick on me and tease me. I felt hopeless at times because I didn't have any brothers and no father to protect me. I later realized that I always had a protector in the Lord, who gave me an understanding that I needed to stop hanging with certain individuals. He also gave me the knowledge to get my education. I had to stop focusing on what I didn't have and start focusing on what I did have. Overtime I learned to deal with and succeed despite my father's absence.

Fight Police Brutality

We must admit, brothers, sometimes we give the police a reason to pull us over. Because of what we have experienced with another police officer or with someone else, we have an attitude before the officer even gets out of the car. I know I've been guilty of it in the past.

I've wondered, *Why is he pulling me over?* or *Why is he harassing me?* before he even gets out of the car. My first thought is never, *He could be pulling me over because I'm in danger with a flat tire.or someone just stole a truck that looks like mine or I may have swerved and he wants to make sure I'm not drink -ing.*

Just like many of you, I'm frustrated, *I was going the speed limit, but I'm driv -ing a car that he thinks I can't afford.* I say, *My truck is paid off and I have the title. It's in my name.*

We already expect the worst. In some cases we have a reason to; however, we must be cautious, play it cool just in case we are wrong about everything.

Ways to Prevent Trouble
When Pulled over by the Police

1. **Keep your cool.** Don't give the officer a reason to use excessive force on you, harass you or lock you up. If you cursing them out every time you get pulled over, they have a reason to lock you up. Be as polite as you can at all times. Remember, the officer that pulls you over doesn't know anything about your identity or police record. They may be pulling over someone with a loaded firearm itching to kill a police officer. Don't give them a reason to think you're on their most wanted list, so keep your cool and play it safe. Live to see another day outside of the confines of a jail cell.

2. **Write down their badge number.** Sometimes you may run across a cop who uses his badge to treat you unfairly. That's when you write down his badge number and turn him in or file a complaint.

3. **Keep your hands out in the open** where they can see them to prevent any false pretenses.

4. **Inform the police of your every move.** When you are reaching for something let them know verbally what you are doing. Let them know where your license and registration are before you reach for them. Make sure you store your legal documents where you can reach them right away.

Ways to Prevent Trouble
When Pulled over by the Police (cont.)

5. **Don't smoke weed in your car.** If you are riding in a car blasting your music with three brothers in the front seat and three in the back seat with smoke coming out of the window and your car isn't on fire, you are giving the police a license to harass you. Be smart. Don't make the situation worse. You shouldn't smoke weed in the first place, but that's your choice, just keep it off the road.

6. **Don't curse at the police** when they pull you over. If you are not guilty, fight your battle in court. If you are guilty, accept that you've been caught. Stand up and face the consequences.

Fight the Powers of Brothers being Violent

Back in 1992, two young men became angry with each other over a young lady and got into an argument in a high school cafeteria. The two young men were best friends at the time. One of them became furious and stabbed the other in the neck with a plastic knife from the cafeteria and the young man died on the scene in front of everyone. Two young men were lost that day. One was killed, while the other went to prison for the rest of his life. There was no chance of reconciliation.

Please understand that when you make quick decisions to do something, you may regret it the rest of your life. When you kill someone, death is final. This young man found out the hard way. Now he is living in a prison cell the rest of his life wishing he hadn't killed his best friend. He didn't mean to kill him, but if you stab someone in the neck the right way, you are bound to hurt or kill that person.

This story inspired me to teach because I knew that teaching would give me the platform and the audience that I needed to help create change. I didn't know I would end up teaching at Arlington High School in Indianapolis, the same high school where this horrible incident between the two young men took place. At Arlington, I felt like I was more of a counselor than a teacher because students constantly came to me with life changing problems that they needed solutions to.

That young man had been in prison for several years. I remember when I first heard his story. I was in college at the time when he appeared on the Oprah Winfrey Show via satellite from prison. He discussed the details of the tragic events. Reliving that day was not easy for him. I guess when you are sitting in prison for the rest of your life, you have a lot of time on your hands to think. He stated that he wished the situation would have turned out differently. His violent rage for one moment changed his whole life. He talked about his future and how different it would have been if he would have fought his best friend instead of stabbing him that day. Maybe they would have been college roommates and laughed about the whole incident later. But as things stand, that option will never be possible.

What happened to the old school way of knuckling up and fighting like men? Fist fights seem to be a thing of the past in our society. I am good friends with a lot of guys I fought growing up. We had disagreements that sometimes turned into fights, but we laugh about it now because we understand that we were kids back then. Young men these days don't fight. If they talk strong to you, you better believe they have a weapon or several guys standing nearby to back them up.

Why not fight and live to see another day? When I was a kid, Carlos Jefferson, a neighborhood friend and I used to fight from time to time, but today we are good friends. I even fought with my good friend Herb Dove when we were kids, but I was one of the groomsmen in his wedding a few years ago. We all graduated from the same high school together. Carlos was on the wrestling team, while Herb played basketball and I played football. My sisters were friends with their sisters and still are.

A lot of young people today can't say that. Far too many of our boys are spending time in prison, instead of the classroom or with their families. I know there are some bad people out there and you may feel like you have to protect yourself, but everyone is not out to get you. Young men think about what you are doing before you pull that trigger. It will change your life forever.

I have been in fights my whole life and I'm not going to let anyone push me around, but I have learned to walk away from conflict. It took time, but I had to learn the hard way. I used to think that standing up and fighting showed how tough I was, but it really was showing how weak I was. Real men walk away from negative conflict, not toward it.

Ways to Prevent a Violent Rage

1. Don't be so quick to anger. When you're faced with a confrontation remind yourself to stay calm. Control your emotions. If you stay under control, the situation is bound to end on a positive note even if the other person is not.

2. Before you confront someone, speak with a friend, family member or mentor who can give you sound, unbiased advice.

3. Don't be so prone to violence right away. Decide to use violence only in extreme circumstances where you are in danger. Otherwise be mature enough to walk away. Walking away is tough, but it's the right thing to do and the safest.

If you do decide to get a gun, go downtown to get an application to get your gun permit. Go to the firing range and learn how to use your weapon properly and only use it if someone is threatening your life, not when you get mad at someone. After you get the permit, take your gun to get it registered so you can carry it legally. It's that simple. I have a license to pack a gun now, but I don't even carry it.

Fight the Powers of Carrying Illegal Weapons

Too many young people today don't fight anymore. Guns and knives are their solutions to small problems. They use a permanent solution for a temporary problem. Guys pull out their illegal guns to fight battles. Many cases every year go unsolved and I see one brother after the next die in the streets from gunshot wounds from untraceable guns; the person who did it is usually never brought to justice. There are trigger happy people in our society who have no regard for their own life or anyone else's. If you have this mentality, you are asking for a date with death and destruction. Guns are dangerous and if you don't have the right attitude, you shouldn't own one.

Picture a young thug riding around with his friends—loaded guns in the car and no gun permit. Now imagine another brother with a loaded gun, a bad attitude and no permit and another waiting for someone to look at him the wrong way so he can try out the gun he just bought up the block for less than $50. I know many guys that took this path. Because the before mentioned boys wanted to prove how tough they were, they ended up in jail for gun possession. Is that the life you want to live, spending 50-100 years behind bars?

Aiming illegal guns at innocent people and showing off for friends is not going to get you anywhere but in trouble. There are too many young people today, riding around town in their cars with loaded guns. The gun charge you get while you are a juvenile can mess you up in your later life when you are going after that big job.

You can buy a gun on the street like candy now. Just recently five basketball players were gunned down at a college party over a girl. Two ignorant losers came to the party with loaded guns looking for trouble and gunned down five young men who were only out to have a good time; college students trying to get their education.

I have seen the destruction that guns have brought to our society and to my personal life. I've seen how it has destroyed young black men in general, including my cousin and my two best friends. How many of your friends have you lost to gun violence? As men, we have to find a way to put the guns down and walk away in peace.

There is too much killing going on. I understand feeling the need to carry a gun, however it's not the right decision. I have been there and done that. When I got angry, the first thing I wanted to do was pull my gun out. I was one of those young brothers who carried an illegal gun for years with no permit. It's wrong. Only by the grace of God did nothing happen to ruin my life. I have shot at people in the past when my temper was not under control, but God spared me and the other person. You may not be as fortunate. Don't take that risk. It's not worth it. I was young and immature and shouldn't have carried a gun in the first place. They are not the answer. They only contribute to problems.

Sometimes you are put in bad situations. I know I put myself in bad situations. One time I was hanging out with some friends and they were shooting at cans. I joined in. What if someone had walked in the path and caught a stray bullet, it would have been my fault. I understand that you want to feel safe wherever you go, but remember the choice to carry a weapon is yours. If you get caught up in a bad situation where you shoot someone and injure or kill them, stand up and be a man and take your punishment. Don't make excuses about why you ended up in the situation.

When I carried a gun as a teenager, I blamed it on my old neighborhood and how I grew up fearing for my life. That was the only excuse I could come up with. The truth was I carried a gun because I chose to carry one. I put my gun down when I chose to let God lead my path, and when I began to trust him with my life. If someone tries to rob you or breaks into your home, you have every right to protect yourself by any means. If you are threatened or provoked to use your gun, you have justification to use it, therefore register your gun. At any rate, make the right choice for your life.

Fighting Racism in Public

I have experienced being mistreated and discriminated against in restaurants and department stores. I've even walked out and taken my money to another restaurant because of being treated unprofessionally and disrespectfully. I had that choice. You also have a choice. When you are spending your hard earned money you can spend it anywhere you want and any way you want to spend it. Just remember that where you spend your money is more powerful than patronizing the same establishment that doesn't appreciate your business. Instead of losing your cool, show some class, walk away and hit them where it hurts by patronizing their competition.

CHAPTER 8

Consequences of Living a "Thug Life"

"I tried to told you um thug," is how Jay Z begins his rhyme on one of hit raps. *I'm a Thug* is the title of one of Trick Daddy's rap hits. Tupac's CD titled *Thug Life*, idolizes the thug lifestyle. Why does everyone want to be a thug?

I have watched real thugs rise and fall, so I don't really understand the logic. The dictionary states that a thug is a brutal hoodlum or gangster. Nowadays the personification of the thug, including being flashy with material possessions, such as gaudy, super-sized jewelry, over-priced automobiles, lavish homes and women who look like models, has a strong hold on our young black men. The hoodlums of the past were afforded these luxuries because of their illegal activity. Today a greater number of black males have gained wealth through professional athletics and in the music industry. Most of these young men with new wealth, once they are able to afford a better lifestyle have begun to express their newfound social status the same way thugs from their neighborhood did. This expression, mixed with the glorification of the thug in videos, has cause a generation of young wealthy black men who conduct their affairs and live their lives patterned after the common thug.

Although they are in the position to affect positive change, they are lost. Blind, uneducated leaders, they flaunt their wealth and power, influencing young brothers to chase after their lifestyle. Those who lack the perseverance to finish school or lack athletic ability or lyrical talent, find themselves caught up selling drugs and illegal weapons, robbing and stealing all in pursuit of the lifestyle that their celebrity idols portray, not realizing that it all goes back to the thug that the celebrity idolized when he was a child.

I grew up in a neighborhood where thuggin' was admired and drug activity was heavy. Young black men in my neighborhood including myself looked up to the thugs. We didn't have fathers, so since the thugs seemed to have all the money and muscle, we wanted to be like them, watching and wishing. It seemed that they lived a stress free life with no worries.

I found out later that it wasn't true. It's actually a life of stress and strife to say the least; a life of hope and dreams being shattered. It's a life where men turn on their best friends and murder them over drugs and money. Best friends testify against each other in court and some don't make it in to testify because they were found dead the night before the trail.

I didn't see men in business suits in my neighborhood and most young men growing up this way don't. I only witnessed families struggling to get by. Most of my friends' parents had blue collar jobs in factories or worked construction or at restaurants. When I thought about how my family was struggling, I figured that living the thug life could be our way out of the hood. I thought that if I listened to the hustlers in my neighborhood, not only would I get money, but I would also get women and respect too. I was wrong.

Those same guys that I looked up to started dropping like flies, at young ages. One died after the other and it continued to happen. I was going to far too many funerals. Those who didn't die in the streets went to prison to serve major sentences for selling drugs and committing other crimes. The judge would give them time without blinking. At the end of each trial and after the funerals, everyone just moved on with their lives and kept living. That's when I started to realize that the "thug life" wasn't for me. I wasn't ready to die or spend the rest of my life in prison.

How do we convince our young men not to be seduced by this life? They see it on BET and MTV everyday in the videos and the messages the videos represent. I look back and remember how I believed the images I saw on TV. Women loved the tough guys and gravitated to the Thugs and I wanted to be one. I wanted to carry a gun and look hard. I wanted to be feared and loved at the same time. My mom always told me that the images I saw were false, but I didn't understand at the time. She encouraged me to work hard and get a job and do it the right way and not follow in the footsteps of the thugs in my neighborhood. She told me that all those guys in my neighborhood doing it that way wouldn't last and she was right. Whether it was by death, prison or becoming strung out on drugs, none of them made it. They had wealth and status temporarily just as she said. She told me if I didn't work for the things I wanted, I didn't deserve nor need them.

Many young brothers are dying all across the country and no one seems to really care. Just like with so many other black male victims, the murders of my two best friends have yet to be solved. Statistics of young black men dying have risen over the last five years.

I have watched over thirty of the guys from my neighborhood go to their graves far too soon and watched thirty or more go to prison. I used to keep a list. I stopped counting after thirty. If that is what the thug life represents, we need to reevaluate ourselves as black men for chasing after a lifestyle that leads to death or incarceration. Our young black boys need to witness more men of God. They need to see more images of positive, successful black men who are not just ball players and entertainers.

If the media doesn't introduce them to us, then we have to be willing to do it ourselves. We have to go to where these lost young men are whether it's the school or the street corners. Show up for their career day in their schools, speak or organize a roundtable discussion in your area with the boys and men from your community. This can be done at your local church. Invite them to your organizations' meetings, so they can see what real men look like and how they conduct business. They don't know what they can become until they are exposed to alternatives to the glorified thug life.

Thug Life in Pro Sports and Rap Music

Athletes are in the news all the time for trying to live the "thug life." The NFL has gotten tougher on rules for players who continue to get in trouble. Over the past few years, three suspensions were handed down to NFL players for their conduct off the field. One player received the most severe penalty handed down by being the first player in NFL history to be suspended for a whole season for his conduct off the field. Over the past few years, he had been arrested ten times. This professional athlete threw over $80,000 in cash on the floor of a strip club causing a riot where one man was shot and paralyzed. He said that he wanted to make it rain, referring to the rap song by Fat Joe and Lil Wayne about having so much money to waste that it is no big deal to throw it in the air and watch it come down like rain.

Another player was arrested and sentenced to jail on gun charges when several unregistered guns were found at his home. As if that weren't enough, he was also out at a nightclub when an altercation broke out where his main body guard was shot to death. Because of his troubles with the law, he was sentenced to jail. The NFL had already suspended him for eight games, but he was still allowed to play in the Super Bowl loss against the Colts. After he was released from jail, he was pulled over again for drinking and driving. This time the Bears made a bold move and cut him.

Players are now being held at a higher standard and they should be. Kids look up to them whether they like it or not. Maybe now that the penalties have become stiffer these young athletes will be forced to take more responsibility for their actions.

Some of our most famous music personalities have spent time in prison after making it big in the rap game. Some of them feel it personifies their toughness and gives them street credibility. The only thing it gives them is lost time for doing something stupid. Unfortunately, these are the role models our young people look up to and aspire to be like.

The Down Side of the Thug Life

There is nothing fun about being shot. I have never been shot, but have several friends who have and most of them didn't live to brag about how it felt. When that bullet hit them, their lives ended. However, I do have some friends who survived being shot and I heard the total opposite from them. Being shot humbled them and they decided to turn away from a life of being thugs. They saw their lives flash before them and decided to live the right way. I had some close calls myself and it made me look at things differently and appreciate my life.

It's sad that some of our young men will not get it until it's too late. Some of them will continue to live this thug life until it takes them out. Many of my friends chose to be thugs, but found out shortly afterward it was a short lived life. Even if you are the toughest in your neighborhood, someone is going to come after you eventually to take you out. Every major champion in sports, including

Michael Jordan, Muhammad Ali and Jerry Rice were the best in their sports, but eventually each of them lost their position to another rising star. Age caught up with them. You can't stay at the top forever.

The same holds true for the tough guys in the neighborhood. They will only reign for so long before someone else goes for their position and it's usually someone either already in their camp or close to them. Whether they take you out by death or incarceration, it will leave an opportunity for someone else to move into the spotlight.

When I taught high school, I remember hearing young men speak about being locked up and bragging about it like it was a great accomplishment. What's cool about spending time in jail or prison? I think I missed it somewhere. You are being told what to do,when, and how to do it. Your freedom is taken away from you and you're around men 24 hours a day. That alone is enough to deter me. I like being around my male friends, but not 24 hours a day. I like using the restroom in privacy. I like going to work without someone breathing down my back. I like getting up to open my front door to my house when I get ready to get some fresh air. I enjoy going to the movies or going out to eat when I want to. I don't like being confined. Moving around on my own fits me. In jail, you have to follow rules. In my home, I make the rules, but I follow God's principles.

Athletes are Targets for Thugs

A basketball superstar went to a night club in New York City one evening with a $50,000 gold chain around his neck. After he proceeded to leave the club, some guys waited for him and snatched his necklace from his neck and shot a notable rapper in his leg as they fled the scene. The basketball player was not shot, but it was a close call. He had grown up in the streets of New York in the projects, so he was used to being around drug dealers and thugs, so he felt comfortable in their company.

He failed to realize when he signed that multi-million dollar contract he was not one of them anymore. He soon learned that when you are making millions of dollars in the NBA, you have to separate yourself from your so called friends and be more careful about where you go and the company you keep. It's not about selling out or forgetting where you came from. It's about adapting to a lifestyle different from the one you were accustomed to growing up in, with no money.

There comes a time in a young man's life when it's obvious that some of your friends need to go. You know they are not trying to get to the same level you are reaching for. The elevator is going to the top floor, but most of your friends will not be able to make the ride. They are not ready for the upcoming challenges and the level you are trying to get to, so let them go. Many guys I grew up with, I had to let go of because I didn't want a life consisting of hanging out on the corners drinking and smoking. It's ok to have your hood in your heart, but be smart about it.

Be Smart and Live to See Another Day

I'm not proud of some of the things I went through growing up. Reliving some of those moments makes me have nightmares. It wasn't fun being jumped by four strangers on my way to the candy store or on my way to the bus stop in the morning before school. It wasn't fun being robbed on my paper route when my collection book was forced out of my hands in broad day light by ten or eleven guys that I knew from my neighborhood. When they approached me and told me to give it up, I didn't hesitate because I knew my life depended on it. Stop trying to be Mr. Toughguy when someone has a gun or knife to your head or neck trying to take your stuff. It's not worth it. You can get more stuff, but you can't get more you.

I surrendered my collection book to those guys, which mostly all are dead or in jail now. I know that I made the right decision because if I didn't, I probably wouldn't be here discussing it today. When I was approached by them to give my book up, I just gave it up. I knew most of the guys and all of them were involved in some illegal activities and I didn't want to make the list so I let them have it. I hid in the bushes and watched those guys collect my money from my customers. It was tough to watch, but at age eleven I decided it was healthier to just go on with my life. I figured they were going to pay for what they did in their own time.

Many wanna be thugs feel they have to prove themselves, so they entertain the risk when approached with danger. Your jewelry and money is not enough to lose your life over. These thugs will kill you over your stuff. If someone is threatening your wife and kids, that's a different story, but the material things are not worth losing your life over. Proving your manhood has a time and place.

Gone Too Soon

Tupac Shakur, my favorite rapper of all time, and Biggie are both dead because they tried to live the life they portrayed in their music. Someone asked Biggie back in the early 90's where he saw himself in ten years and he said, "Probably dead." If you continue to speak it into existence, it's bound to happen. He died a horrible death during the early morning hours in Los Angeles in 1997.

Tupac was gunned down in Vegas just one year prior to Biggie in a convoy of cars and no admitted to having seen anything? These two talented brothers were true poets who perfected their craft. Biggie didn't write rhymes. He memorized his whole album without writing down a single lyric. Both were millionaires and very talented artists. They used to be friends, but it turned into an all out war between east and west coast by the time their lives ended causing more killing and less uniting.

Rap and Hip Hop is a huge part of our culture, but somehow rap music is getting more and more violent encouraging our young men to do the same. We kill each other over trivial conflicts. When Tupac and Biggie died, they both had put out enough music to last for the next ten years.

Both rappers wrote about dying in many of their songs and died the thug way they portrayed in their music. What good is it doing them now? These young talented brothers are dead because they wanted to be thugs. It doesn't make sense.

The Choice is Yours

Some brothers seem to have a crab in the bucket mentality. As soon as a brother is trying to give up that thug life and get his life together, another brother pulls him down by reminding him of what he used to do in the past. Many guys are trying to walk away from this life, so encourage them to continue to do so.

When you see a man in a suit, don't assume he is soft because you might be mistaken. You don't know what that man has gone through to be where he is today or the life he left behind. Young men need to see professional black men instead of of grown men sagging their jeans like they see on the videos. Many of us grew up fighting and getting into trouble until we matured into men. I made a choice to change the cycle and leave the mischief behind. I made a choice to not be like the other thugs in my neighborhood even though at times I did act like them. There is no way I can help another young man if I don't share my story with him and be truthful about how far I've come and how far I have to go.

Our young men are being raised to fight if someone looks at them wrong. I was the same way. If someone crossed me, I had that thug mentality and my first reaction was to fight or have some kind of confrontation with them and that's not the right way to go. That is the main reason so many of our young black men are dead today.

Walking away from confrontation makes us men. At times in the past, I wasn't capable of doing that. At times, even as an adult, it's still challenging. I'm a father myself now and I have to lead by example. I notice that my son watches every thing I do. As we say in 100 Black Men, "What they see is what they will be." If you handle conflicts by fighting, your son will fight. If you handle conflicts by walking away, your son will be more prone to walk away.

Doing the right thing has its price. I remember going through a phase of loneliness. I felt like I didn't have any friends. When you choose to change your life from running around with the thugs and gang bangers, many people you used to run with will not be happy about it. After I stopped hanging with those guys, some of them gave me a hard time, ridiculing me. Sometimes they even ganged up on me.

Either you are a follower or a leader. Make the choice because that's what it boils down to. I had to stop hanging with certain people who were pulling me down and I knew there was a cost for that. The pain I went through was tough, but I made it through the tough time and I'm still here and very successful at what I do. My coaches used to tell me in high school and college that in order to become a champion, you have to endure some pain. Stop thinking because you decided not to be a thug or drug dealer anymore that it's going to be an easy transition because it's not.

Those same guys that you called your friends are going to stab you in the back. They are going to talk about you because you are no longer one of them. Some may even go into a jealous rage and try to fight you or hurt you. Whatever the case may be, stay the course. It's your choice to go back to that life or to start over doing it the right way. You may have scars that remind you of where you came from, but that's ok. I have plenty of scars that remind me of my past, but it's still my past but they continue to heal, reminding me just how far I've come.

The After Affects

Unless you have lived in that type of environment or know of someone who did, you probably can't relate. Some people don't understand how it affects you. I went to college to get my degree; played sports, graduated on time, but my life was still affected. I still attended my friend's funerals, even in college and experienced the same pain over and over. With all that I've accomplished, I'm still haunted by my past.

I'm blessed to still be alive. In the past I have been involved in altercations trying to prove myself and almost ended up dead or in jail. I still didn't get it. I thought because I decided not to kill anyone or sell drugs or rob a bank, that I was cool. I didn't know that every time I got into a fight that it could potentially be fatal for me and my family. I thought because I was still going to school that I was going to be find. I was right to a certain extent.

It's good to go to school and get your education, but if you bury things, eventually those things will come to the surface. Deal with the pain of your past by talking about it. If you harmed someone, apologize to them and their families. Understand that the family may not receive you, but if you asked God for forgiveness and tried to make it right with the family, you have done your part.

One bad decision changes everything

I knew a young man who never got in trouble in his life. He had gone to college and got his degree and was married with two kids working hard to take care of his family. He never had any trouble with the law.

One day, he was propositioned by a guy he had just met through some friends who was looking for someone to connect with to make a drug deal. Even though he couldn't help the guy personally, he grew up in an environment similar to the environment I grew up in. We didn't sell drugs, but we knew the people who did.

The deal was too good to be true. He was offered $100,000 if he could connect this guy with someone who carried the right amount of drugs. He didn't know at the time, but the guy he was conversing with was an informant working for the FBI.

He was blinded by the money. He had a chance to make $100,000 off of one deal just for hooking this guy up with the right person. He knew it would only take a quick phone call and he could walk away with $100k with no problem. Even though it was risky, he decided to take the guy up on his offer. He contacted one of his friends who had the product this guy was looking for and set a date for the deal.

Remember, this guy had never been in trouble for anything in his life. When the deal went down, the FBI was there to apprehend his friend he hooked the informant up with. Even though he wasn't there during the deal, he went down for setting everything up. He went to trial and his friend was there also. At this point, his friend thought that he was a snitch who set him up, so his friend wanted him dead.

After a short trial, the judge sentenced the man who set up the deal to 35 years in prison, fed time. Fed time means you do 85% of your time. This was the least amount of time that he could receive because of the amount of drugs involved. That's how quick your life can change, young men. This guy lived a straight life all the way up to his 30th birthday and got caught up in some mess that he shouldn't have been a part of in the first place. Those few moments cost him 35 years of his life. He won't be eligible to get out of jail until he is 60 years old.

He lost his good job, his wife and two kids and threw it all away for the love of money and a quick dab into the thug lifestyle that he avoided for so many years. He made a deal with the devil and lost. It's a sad story, but very true. The decisions you make can affect your whole life. I bet he wishes he could take that deal back, but he can't.

Money is necessary to provide and bills have to be paid, but being led by excessive materialism is a trap that can easily lead you down a path of crime and other illegal activity. Our young men are being led by materialism in the media and their neighborhoods. The guys in the hood with all the money are usually the thugs. Money can buy you a lot, but can't buy you a good night's rest, a good appetite, a peace of mind, your health or a ticket into heaven.

Do Your Part

If we would grab these young thugs and encourage them to stand up and change their ways, we can make a difference. We have to do more than talk about it. We need to teach them how to talk and how to dress and how to act because they haven't been taught. It's our responsibility to teach these young men how to prepare for job interviews. It's our responsibility to share our experiences with these young men in hopes that it will deter them from wanting to live this kind of life. They need to know that the right way is through God and through loving each other and themselves. We must lead by example. There are consequences for living this kind of life, but it's not too late for them to change.

It's sad to see our young men idolize a lifestyle that constantly causes pain. A lifestyle that is responsible for the thousands upon thousands of deaths of our young black brothers. It's the reason why so many of our young men disrespect the women in their lives. It's a major reason for black on black crime.

Many of us go to work everyday, make our money, go back home and don't reach out to mentor one young man. We complain all the time about young men sagging their pants, but don't teach or encourage them to pull them up. We complain all day about how young men sell drugs, but don't offer them jobs.

We are more concerned with how much money we are making and watering our grass in our nice big suburban home. We are more concerned with going to our social clubs to stick our chest out and make ourselves seem bigger than what we are. Young men hang on street corners all day long, while we drive right through their neighborhoods without stopping or showing concern for their well-being.

I'm not putting the full blame on us as men, but we are a big part of the problem because not enough of us are stepping up to the plate to contribute to a solution. Some men are doing a great job of mentoring, but as a whole, we need more men involved in the lives of our young men as positive role models.

Maybe we have forgotten how crazy we used to act when we were younger. Maybe we have forgotten that a lot of us barely made it out of the hood alive. So why is it so hard for you to give back to other young brothers who don't have a clue? We can't change how we grew up or the circumstances we faced, but we can be a positive influence for them. They need to hear our stories and how we changed our lives. They need to hear about our downfall and how we rose above poverty and destruction to be who we are today. We can't just walk by and let them make the same mistakes we made.

When we discuss rap music we need to tell these young black boys the truth about the videos and life of rappers. They need to know that the rap lyrics tell a story just like movies and some movies are real and some aren't. They need to know that the material possessions seen in the videos, like the cars, jewelry, clothes and money are rented and not owned by most of these rappers. They need to know that those models in the videos are hired to be there. They need to know that every rapper is not a gangster, but an artist expressing a version of their story that is not always reality based.

Our young men need to be encouraged that God loves them and spared them for a reason. They need to know all of their so-called friends aren't really friends. They need to be encouraged that dropping out of school to hustle is a bad decision no matter how good the money looks. We have to explain their history to them so they understand where we came from and the struggles we experienced to be here today. It is up to us as men to counter negative influence and teach our young men to lead and not follow.

It's obvious that they are misguided and have been led astray, but it's our responsibility to lead our young men in the right direction. Just let them know you care. Be consistent. When you say you are going to do something, do it. If you say you are going to give them a ride to a job interview, make sure you do it. If you are going to teach, teach. If you are going to coach, coach. If you are going to be a mentor, mentor. Just let them know you care about them and that you want to see them become successful. It may take some time to sink in, but if you are being persistent, they'll get it. Not all of them will listen and some will be lost, but if you save one, you have done your part.

CHAPTER 9

ABUSE
(Are Brothers Using Some Excuse?)

I ask you, "Are brothers using some excuse for abusive behavior?" Were you abused as a child? Did you watch your mom experience abuse physically or verbally? Are you scared of giving your heart to one woman because of what you saw your father do to your mother? Did your father run the streets with different women while you rode in the back seat of the car witnessing his infidelity? Do your friends tease you when you talk about committing to one woman? Did someone violate you? Were you sexually assaulted and too embarrassed to talk about it? Are your parents divorced and you blame yourself? Did your babysitter take advantage of you when you were a child? Was there no man around to teach you how to be a man and how to treat a woman?

I will not make excuses for brothers abusing women or each other because we individually have to take responsibility for our own actions whether or not we grew up experiencing or witnessing abuse. Just because I experienced abuse, doesn't mean I have to continue to live my life abusing. Some men hold on to the abuse they experienced for so long, that they bury it in the back of their minds and don't deal with it, thinking it's gone forever, but it comes out in their actions and their speech and the way they treat others.

Many of us, including myself, who have lived with the hurt from past abuse far too long attempt to bury the pain in hopes that no one will find out the truth. Some men talk about the other brothers who are being real with their woman.

They hate on them calling them weak. Others don't let anyone close to their hearts, letting the "good girls" pass them by. I know how it feels to hurt. I know how it feels to hold on to emotions that you want to express to someone, but you keep balled up inside, hoping no one will ever find out. It eats away at you and tears you up inside. As a result, you hurt other people around you that care about you.

Abuse can come in many forms, whether it's sexual, physical, verbal, or neglect. It is also a tough topic to discuss. Men tend to have egos so they prefer not to talk about it. To most, speaking about past abuse is embarrassing and often demoralizing. Many men who abuse women have been victims of abuse themselves or have watched their moms being abused by her husband or boyfriend. How do you tell your wife that another man touched you, attempted to have sex with you or raped you? How would someone explain it to their girlfriend or significant other that their babysitter had molested them over and over from the time they were four years old? It wouldn't be easy to do and many men and women take those dreadful memories to their graves, destroying or at the very least making miserable their lives and the lives they connect with.

Overcoming Sexual Abuse

I truly admire Laverananeus Coles for his courage to come forward on Oprah Winfrey's show. The tears rolled down his mom's face as he told his story in front of millions of viewers. She couldn't believe what her son had gone through. Coles, who currently plays wide receiver in the NFL, shared that he had been sexually abused at gun point by his step-father for more than nine years, dating back when he was a child. Coles had held on to this nightmare for years until one of his high school classmates called him gay. In an angry rage he beat his classmate so bad that he had to be restrained by several people. Coles began screaming out of control and no one knew what was wrong. All of his emotions were running wild because he had kept all of that anger bundled inside for years. Can you imagine being a child and having a man come to your room night after night behind your mom's back, placing a gun to your head and forcibly having sex with you against your will?

He inspired me to come forward and speak out about my abuse. I hadn't been able to bring myself to talk about it before because I was embarrassed. It was bad enough that I was constantly being teased by other kids in my neighborhood for being an only boy with four sisters. As an adult I had suppressed it, put it behind me and never spoke of it because I didn't want to be reminded of things from my childhood that hurt me. I can relate to Coles because I hid behind sports also. I was so young when it happened and vaguely remember everything so my attitude was, why talk about it? I had an image to uphold. I didn't want to be looked down on as weak.

When I was seven or eight years old, I was molested by one of my aunt's boyfriends. He called two of my sisters and me into a room one by one and fondled us. I remember like it was yesterday and didn't understand at the time exactly what was taking place. I knew something was wrong, but wasn't old enough to realize or articulate what happened. It was so long ago and I don't remember why I didn't tell my mom. My sisters never spoke of it either. I don't remember if he threatened us, but we never spoke about it. I thought about it from time to time, but didn't know where to begin. I didn't know how to approach my sisters either. When I finally asked them about it, they said they didn't remember. They acted as if it never took place, but I know it did. I can see it like it happened yesterday minus some details. They probably blocked it out. As I got older, I knew it was wrong and it angered me. I never knew what happened to that guy, but never forget how empty I felt.

There are some sick people in the world and it's not a child's fault if they are molested or abused. However, internalizing such traumatic incidents and never releasing the pain can dramatically affect your adult relationships. If left unaddressed, the baggage you carry stays the same when going from relationship to relationship. Until it's released, problems will continue to follow. Once it's released, it doesn't have the same control over you.

Overcoming Physical Abuse

As a child, I was also physically abused and watched my mom get verbally and physically abused as well. My mom and I have always been close. When I was a kid, I used to wait up for her to come home from work. I would fall asleep by the door and when she came home, the door would hit me in the back, waking me up. My mom's boyfriends didn't like the fact that I waited up for her and was jealous of our relationship.

He made my life miserable. An alcoholic, he was always loud and abusive when he drank, especially toward me and my oldest sister. He was a Vietnam veteran who hallucinated quite often about the Vietnam War. Sometimes he would wake up screaming "They are right over there." He would grab his gun and point it as he repeatedly yelled at an invisible person.

One particular night, he had been drinking heavily. He didn't want me waiting up for my mom. I was only five or six years old. He repeatedly told me to go to bed, yelling and screaming at the top of his lungs.

As his voice escalated and his posture became more threatening, I began to stand up to go to my room, but it was too late. This man who stood 6'4" and weighed over 240 pounds, immediately grabbed me by my shirt and raised me off the ground with his fist under my chin. He took me to the doorway of my bedroom and threw me across the room where I hit the wall, then the bed. Before I bounced up off the bed from the throw, he turned around and walked out of the room with no remorse slamming the door shut behind him. He didn't even check on me to see if I was okay. He didn't care. I was left in severe pain both from hitting the wall and from his cold hearted treatment.

He would always find ways to pick with my older sister and me behind my mom's back. Sometimes he would smack me in the face for no reason at all and then threaten me saying, "You better not tell your mother."

My sister and I were the darkest of my other three siblings. I always felt that was the reason. Other times he would push me around because he was bigger than I was.

Verbal abuse was a daily routine with him. He loved to do it when my friends were around. One time he embarrassed me by coming out in the street grabbing me while my friends and I were playing football. He yelled and cursed at me for no reason telling me to cut the grass. Earlier that day, he had told me I could cut the grass the next day. He had been drinking heavily and forgot what he told me earlier. I felt totally disrespected in front of my boys. I hated that man.

He would never lift me up or praise any of my successes. I excelled in school and sports, but he never recognized me, but always found a way to put me down. He eventually got caught in his own insanity when he tried to rape his own daughter. My mom left him.

When I was about ten or eleven my mother started seeing another guy. He had three daughters of his own, so when he found out my mom had four daughters, he took to them quickly, but never gave me a chance. He was on me about every little thing I did and never encouraged me.

When I was fourteen, he came into my room with a joint rolled up. I had never touched the stuff before. I was an athlete. He lit it up and told me to take a hit. I asked him what he meant and he proceeded to show me how to smoke it. I took one hit and began to cough out of control. He laughed as I bent over, attempting to catch my breath.

He would go out of the house and stay gone for days at a time and then come home and disrespect my mother, right in front of me, yelling and screaming, acting as if he did nothing wrong. I despised him for that. When I was eleven or twelve he had come home really late and had been drinking heavily. My mom was fed up and very upset and repeatedly asked him where he had been. I was awakened by their arguing. Half asleep, I went into the kitchen where he had his hands around my mom's neck choking her. I was only 115 pounds at the time and he was 6'3," 240 pounds. He turned toward me with anger in his eyes and punched me in my face like I was another man and I hit the floor. As I grabbed my jaw, which had already begun to swell, he walked out.

I told my friends about it the next day and I wanted to hurt him bad. I confided in them about how I was going to do it. The anger that I felt for him lingered long after the swelling of my jaw went down. I couldn't wait to confront him. I told myself that I would be ready next time. I wanted him dead and was plotting how I was going to kill him.

He stayed away for a while. By the time he resurfaced again, I had calm down some. My mom encouraged me not to retaliate. I left it alone, although I never forgot or let go of the hurt and anger. He never touched me again.

I had just moved back into my mom's house from Los Angeles after unsuccessful try-outs with the Raiders and Rams. It was my rookie year and I had graduated from college. I didn't know that he had started using drugs and was stealing things around the house to support his habit. I went to play one of my favorite CD's and realized that several of them were missing. I was tipped by my brother-in-law to check a record store near the house. When I went to the record store to check on my stolen CD's, I recognized his handwriting. He had signed the receipt, "Billy the Kid." I had to buy each of my CD's back from the record store.

I was very upset and to make matters worse, when I confronted him about it, he pulled a knife from his pocket and pointed it in my direction. This time I stood my ground, but my mom jumped in front of me. My emotions were raging out of control and all I could think of was taking my gun and blowing him away.

I packed my stuff and moved out that day and never spent another night in that house. I really didn't have anywhere to go at that time, but I knew I couldn't stay there. You don't have to stay in an abusive situation. It may not be easy to leave, but love yourself enough to get out!

Holding on to my anger toward him took its toll on me. I found myself getting upset about the smallest things and would get into altercations with others.

Ways to Cope with Past Abuse

1. **Understand that it wasn't your fault.** Stop blaming yourself. Remember that you were a victim, so stop beating up yourself.

2. **Seek counseling.** Seek professional help. Talk with a psychologist or a counselor at a crisis center to learn the techniques to release past hurts and to help develop healthy relationships.

3. **Talk to someone about it.** Talk to family members, friends, coaches or anyone else you may trust. Speaking with someone about your pain helps you to release it from your system and cope. Don't take your former abuse out on your mate. Tell them what happened to you and if your relationship is real they should be more than happy to lend an ear. If not, they aren't the person you should be with anyway.

4. **Forgive your offender.** Anyone who harmed you was apparently emotionally disturbed and more than likely was a helpless victim at one time themselves. Forgiving your attacker releases you from their power over you.

NO MORE EXCUSES: Black Men Stand Up!

It was hard for me to walk away from any confrontation even though I didn't start them. The thought of contributing to black on black crime by not walking away from altercations never crossed my mind. The only thing on my mind was not letting anyone push me around anymore and that the next person who tried was going to pay.

I didn't let anything slide. If someone brought it to me, I was going to handle my business by making them pay. I was angry and hostile. On one occasion, I was at a party over my friend's house. One of his fraternity brothers, who'd had too much to drink was staggering around the party yelling and touching everyone, being annoying. I tried to stay clear of him and went to the kitchen to fix myself a drink when he came up behind me and grabbed my arm. I quickly snatched away from his grip and told him to back away from me. Then he started taunting me saying, "I think I can take you." He was making a scene, being so loud. Others began to notice his childish behavior. I tried my best to ignore him and walk away, but he followed me all around the party triggering my memory of my mom's boyfriend being drunk and throwing me across the room. Then, I thought of when the other one punched me in my face. His vibe was negative and I wasn't in the mood to deal with his behavior and drunkenness. Eventually I was tired of his ignorance and proceeded to leave the party. I got my jacket and was on my way to my car. I was very angry that he had spoiled my night and I could barely contain myself.

Before I got to my car, I ran into some guys that I knew and began to speak with them, when all of a sudden someone pushed me in my back. I was furious when I turned around and saw the same guy who had been harassing me the whole night. Before I could think, I punched him in his jaw and he flipped over the hood of the car on the side of us. He laid there for a few moments dazed not knowing what hit him. When he started to wake up, he pulled himself up and came toward me again. This time I grabbed my gun and raised it up to smack him in his face when my friend grabbed my arm and asked me to let go of the gun. At that point, I knew I had lost control. I found out later that the guy joined church and never drank again after that night, but it still didn't change the fact that my anger was out of control because of the abuse I had experienced.

One Sunday in church the minister said something that hit home with me and I broke down and all the hurt I had gone through was coming to the surface. I realized that I couldn't get to where God wanted me to be because I was trying to take matters into my own hands. I had a son and wanted to be an example for him. Plus, every time I allowed my anger to guide my actions the situation got worse. The day I surrendered my anger to God was the day I began my healing process. I also improved my defensive attitude and emotional state. I have learned how to ignore, forgive and pray for my enemies and how to have peace and joy instead of anger. Before that, I found myself taking my pain and anger out on others who stepped in my path. After getting it under control, I felt like a new person and people around me started noticing a difference.

Take it from me, if you are holding on to anger from past abuse, it will affect you in your everyday life. When I began to let things go it made me feel better about myself and it will do the same for you. Anger can destroy you before you realize it has a hold on you. There is therapy in speaking about it. There is also power in prayer. Give it to the Lord and you will begin to heal. If you don't deal with it, you'll never have control over your emotions and will make situations worse than what they have to be.

Ways to Control Your Anger

1. Listen, rather than trying to be heard. Hear the other person out and don't outtalk them.

2. Control your voice and tone, remembering that when you increase your volume it increases tension. When the person who you are communicating with raises his or her voice, lower yours and keep it low.

3. Think before you speak. It will prevent you from saying harmful words.

4. When possible, stay away from stressful situations.

5. Learn to forgive those who hurt you.

6. Discover what your limit is and don't cross it.

Too many of us are angry about past hurts and don't know how to release the anger. Love yourself enough to realize that any abuse towards you isn't your fault. Someone else inflicted that pain on you. You can't change what happened to you, but you can control the way you react to it.

Overcoming Verbal Abuse

I don't care how loud a woman talks to you, gets angry or ignores you. Even if she puts her hands on you, which is wrong, she is still the weaker vessel and there is no excuse to abuse her. Women deserve to be treated with respect. Some people believe that names have never hurt anyone, but when that someone has been through some kind of abuse, or has esteem issues, names can be damaging. Yelling and screaming at someone is just as bad as physically touching them. Calling women bitches and whores is no better.

I have grown up my whole life listening to men call women names, like bitches, whores, and sluts. If you hear something long enough, it becomes a part of you and your way of thinking. If you walk through the mall today, you will hear young men referring to other young women by these names and worse. They don't care who's around. At least when we were young and dumb, we respected our elders and didn't say bad things in front of them, but not today's youth.

As a kid I saw adults get into fights, yelling and screaming, so when I got older and had a conflict with my girlfriends, I would yell and scream also, carrying on the same abusive behavior I was accustomed to growing up around. I experienced problems in my past relationships because of my abusive communication style. When things didn't go my way, I just walked away instead of trying to discuss it. When I felt backed into a corner, I yelled and cursed without regard to how my words may have made women feel.

One time I was in the middle of an argument with a young lady that I was dating. We were having a simple discussion that got out of hand because she raised her voice unnecessarily. I felt disrespected so I retaliated. She didn't back down, so I didn't either. Our little discussion turned into a full-blown argument where we both said things that were hurtful. But it wasn't as much what we said, but what I saw when I happened to pass by a mirror while we were having it out. I didn't like what I saw. The anger inside of me was all over my face. The tension in my demeanor was deeper than what we were supposedly arguing about.

At that moment I told myself "You are a man of God and you are not showing it right now."

I remember stopping in my tracks and I told her, the yelling has got to stop and I'm just as guilty as you are. She told me that her parents used to argue back and forth to solve their conflicts. We both were reliving the only way we knew how to solve conflicts. That day for me was the beginning of me changing my way of thinking regarding arguing.

I have continued to keep my word of making a change in that area. It hasn't happened over night. I still yelled, just not as often. Until I was able to completely control my temper, I walked away whenever I caught myself. In later years I learned to meditate on scriptures pertaining to anger and peace and I'm still working on it everyday and I'm so much further along then I used to be.

I do not want to be hurt or hurt anyone else with my words. Yelling and screaming is verbal abuse and it hurts just as bad as physical hurt. I recognize that now, and decided that I'm not going to let the abusive behavior of my past take over me. As men we have to realize when we are at "that point" and try to talk things out calmly or walk away. I know some women continue to yell and scream, that's when you have to be man enough to walk away until she cools off.

I understand all too well that women who refuse to back down make it tough for men who may want to show restraint, but continue on your positive path. Backing down means you are a strong man because it sometimes takes serious restraint not to retaliate when a sister is yelling in your ear. The right thing to do is to remind that sister that you respect her and that it is not necessary for the two of you to go at each other disrespectfully. Be an example. Showing that kind of strength and leadership in a relationship is what it means to be a man.

Moving Forward from Abuse

Don't allow abuse to hold you back from being the kind of man God intended you to be. As hard as it is, we have to face the abuse from our past. Whatever the case may be, talk about it with someone you trust. We think that if we are honest about our deep emotional wounds that others will think we are not being real men. There is nothing wrong with you pouring your heart and soul out to the woman you love, brothers, especially if she gives you no reason not to trust her.

It will more than likely help your relationship. A woman needs to hear the truth to help her understand and become more patient with your behavior or your reactions to conflict.

If you don't trust anyone, talk to God about it. His line is always open day and night. Brothers don't be afraid to seek counseling for the abuse you have dealt with in your past. There are many of us that need counseling for some of the things we have gone through and we need to stop making excuses why we haven't done it yet. Don't hide from your abuse. Stand up brothers and get help now before it's too late.

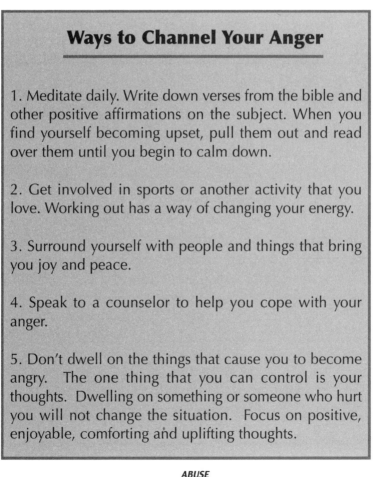

Ways to Channel Your Anger

1. Meditate daily. Write down verses from the bible and other positive affirmations on the subject. When you find yourself becoming upset, pull them out and read over them until you begin to calm down.

2. Get involved in sports or another activity that you love. Working out has a way of changing your energy.

3. Surround yourself with people and things that bring you joy and peace.

4. Speak to a counselor to help you cope with your anger.

5. Don't dwell on the things that cause you to become angry. The one thing that you can control is your thoughts. Dwelling on something or someone who hurt you will not change the situation. Focus on positive, enjoyable, comforting and uplifting thoughts.

CHAPTER 10

Baby Mama Drama

What is Baby Mama Drama? It depends on who you ask. What makes a woman change from Dr. Jeckyll to Mrs. Hyde or vice versa? Is it love or hate? Did you cause it when you were out in the streets cheating on her while she stayed at home with your kids or was she just crazy to begin with? Was the breakup clean or did it cause heartache and pain? Whatever the case may be, the love affair is over and now you have a child by a woman who is causing you more drama than your failed relationship was worth.

Women are fragile creatures and they often wear their feelings on their sleeves. As much as she may get on your nerves, it's not about her. It's about the kids and that should be your focus. While you concentrate on your kids, understand that she may continue to play games with you or cause problems because she is either not totally over you, or you hurt her in some way and she is on a mission to get even. No matter the reason, it's important to be the best father you can be at all times.

Because of baby mama drama, many men are not close to their children. Blaming their absence from their kids' lives on their mom is making an unnecessary excuse, not to mention that it's not fair because the kids suffer.

In some cases women have a right to complain about unfit fathers. When was the last time you saw your child or took him to a ball game. Why aren't you paying your support for your child? What excuses are you making for your irresponsible behavior? Are you being a good role model to your kids?

In other cases, the woman is trying to do anything she can to hurt you. Maybe you flaunted all of your women in her face the whole time you were with her and now she cannot get past it. She is still hurting over your failed relationship and she wants to see you pay. Maybe she caused you trouble on your job as well because she wants to make sure everyone knows that you cheated on her. You are her target and she is not focused on the kids' welfare.

Our children need to learn how to deal with adversity. Any boy can get a woman pregnant, but it takes a man to be a father to those kids. Black men have started a cycle of irresponsibility that's being passed down to our sons and other male members of our families. Brothers, if you give up and throw in the towel, you are teaching your kids to give up also. Is that the message that you want to send to your sons?

We all have fallen short of God's glory. My mom told me a long time ago to be careful who I laid down with. Many of you have heard the same thing, so when you make the decision to have intercourse with the chick you met in the club, you already know that there are consequences to your actions, including the possibility of conceiving a child. We all know the process of getting a woman pregnant, so when you lay down with her, ask yourself, "Am I ready to have a baby with this woman and deal with her the rest of my life?" Because whether you could see yourself involved with her long term or only for the night, once the child is born, he or she is going to need a father. Again, having consensual sex is a choice. Taking care of your children is also a choice which involves stepping up and handling responsibly the results of your actions.

Sometimes it's a broken marriage that didn't work out. You did things the right way, got married and had your family together. It just didn't work out. At any rate, you are stuck with the dilemma of baby mama drama.

Some of you have tried for years to make peace with your kid's mom, but she refuses to be peaceful. That's an internal battle that she is dealing with. Don't allow her to suck you in. Just do your part. You can't make anyone change, but you can change your behavior toward her and how you react to her. Continue to be cordial, pray for her, and make every effort to keep conversations short and focused on the well-being of the kids. Despite your ill feelings toward her, the children must be protected at all times.

Way to Protect Children from the Drama

1. Support them financially. Pay your child support.

2. Be Reliable by showing up on time. When you say you're going to be there or you're going to do something, follow through. If you know you can't keep you promise, don't make one. If you must cancel or reschedule, do so as soon as you can. Children need a sense of security, your reliability can help provide that for them.

3. Spend time with them. Pickup your kids on your scheduled days and on weekends. Go to lunch with them at school and go to PTO meetings.

4. Don't get caught up in unnecessary arguments with your kid's mom. At times conversations turn into loud arguments and you need to avoid these at all costs.

5. Don't say anything bad about your kid's mother in front of them. Even if you have ill feelings toward her, keep them to yourself or confide in someone about it, but keep it away from the kids. Parents don't understand the scars they put on their children when they talk disrespectfully about the other, no matter what they did. It's wrong.

6. Keep conversations with their mother professional and if it goes beyond your child and/or their welfare, cut the conversation short. If you continue to go back and forth between friendly and flirty conversation with the mother, knowing that you don't want the commitment, you are asking for trouble in the long run.

Many of our biological fathers decided to run instead of face their problems with our moms so we suffered. As men, we have to make up in our minds that we are going to be the best fathers we can be despite the obstacles in front of us.

I know so many brothers who get upset with their child's mother and take it out on the child by not spending time with them. Doing so messes things up for them, as well as for the real Christian brothers who are trying to live by God's principals and take care of their responsibilities.

Women know how to use the system to their advantage. A vindictive woman understands that there are more deadbeat dads out there than good fathers and she'll make every effort to get you grouped in the "deadbeat" category. That's why when a good brother who pays child support and spends quality time with their child gets taken to court by a scorned woman, the court is more likely to favor the scorned woman. It's not right that brothers are categorized, but we often are. Don't get discouraged when this happens to you. It has happened to the best of us. Just continue to be consistent with what you are doing for your kids.

If we took a poll of brothers taking care of their kids versus brothers not in their kid's life, where would the numbers fall? You know the answer to that question. If you don't, just ride down the street and watch all of the young men hanging out without the presence of positive male role models. Watch single moms riding the city bus with four or five kids with them.

Some of you say, "It's not my job to take care of my children's mother. She has a husband." Once she gets that check, it's out of your hands, brother. She can spend the whole check on her husband or boyfriend if she wants to and there is nothing that you can do about it. Nonetheless, it is still your legal responsibility to get that check to her.

As men, we should hold unfit fathers accountable. If you have a friend or a relative not taking care of their kids, you should say something to them about it. Good brothers are suffering. Kids are suffering. Our society as a whole is suffering. Let them know they are not only bringing the baby mama drama on themselves, but they are also adding to the turmoil in our families.

Fighting to See Your Children

Although it can sometimes be a lengthy process, men should go to court and fight for their rights to see their children. I hear so many stories about cases against deadbeat fathers. While in court for custody of my son, once the judge gets to me he's already dealt with so many irresponsible men, that he doesn't appear to be as sympathetic to me or any other brothers who are making efforts to care for their children. This can be disheartening to good men who are doing the right thing.

Nonetheless, giving up on our kids because we are not getting along with the mom or not getting what we want from the court system is not the way to go. When it's all said and done we have a responsibility to abide by the rules, no matter what our opinion. Unless you want to make it worse on yourself, don't make excuses just take care of your responsibility. Go to court.

In my custody hearing I felt that the initial ruling was not right, but I didn't give up. I saved my money, found a good attorney and continued to fight my case. When my son's mom would get mad at me, I wasn't allowed to see or speak with him on the phone or in person. I got tired of not being able to communicate with my son and not being able to visit him when I wanted to, so I took it to court. I no longer allowed his mother to dictate when I would see him. When I finished fighting it in court, the judge granted me routine visitation rights.

If you have a child out there somewhere, take care of your child to the best of your ability. There are mothers, like my son's, who try to hurt men through their children, but they really hurt the child. For example, I signed him up to play basketball and I also coached his team. On the days she was scheduled to keep my son, she refused to bring him to his games or his practices so he missed half of his games. She also refused to let me pick him up from her house. She thought she was hurting me, but she was really hurting him. Sports teach discipline and teamwork and she deprived him of that.

On many other occasions my son wanted to call me, but his mom wouldn't allow him because she was trying to hurt me, again she was really hurting him. Keeping fathers from their kids confuses the child and causes them to rebel. No matter what happened between the father and mother, kids love their dads just as much as their moms. Her tactics have taken a toll on my son and that's unfair to him. It bothered me at first, but I decided to let it go and continue to do the best I could for him when I had him. I have come to realize that she is not going

Steps to Fight in the Court System For Visitation Rights

1. **Show up for court.** A lot of black men feel that they are mistreated in the court systems, but you still have to go. Some men choose not to appear on their court dates. You make it worse on yourself when you're not present. How can you challenge the system and fight for your rights if you don't even show?

2. **Pay your child support.** Until the judge rules on your case, you should pay your child support. Why would a judge rule in your favor when you are several months or years behind in your support? If you are behind, catch up.

3. **Fight for visitation.** Some judges are unfair to good fathers because they come across so many deadbeat dads; however, do what you can to get visitation with your kids. They need you. If you lose, you lose with dignity, but not without a fight. Someone depriving you of your rights to your own flesh and blood is like a smack in the mouth, so fight back.

4. **Abide by the rules.** Make them work on your behalf. Many men experience problems with their children's moms being uncooperative, manipulative and disrespectful. As frustrating as it can be, don't fall victim to her games. Keep your cool and remain level headed. Document everything that takes place so you and your attorney can fight the battles in the court room. The court system may not always be friendly to you, but abiding by the rules makes your case stronger.

Steps to Fight in the Court System to See Your Child (Cont.)

5. **Control your temper.** Use your mind in a positive way. Don't let your anger take over. Anger causes too many of us to make the wrong decisions. Instead of doing something or saying something that could later be used against you, create a new strategy to fight back in the only way the court system respects, researching your case, saving your money to get a good attorney, and coming to court on time and prepared. Have all of your paperwork together. Keep a record of all your receipts, child visits and activities you participate in with your child. Document any wrong doings or inappropriate handling of your children by their mothers and others, but above all, keep your cool.

6. **Get involved in your child's life.** Introduce yourself to their teacher. Have lunch with them at their school a few times throughout the year. If possible, volunteer to chaperone at least one or two field trips. If you can't join the PTA, at least attend one open house per year.

7. **Find a job.** If you don't have a job, find one. If you can't find one on your own, go to a temp agency or speak with someone you know who could assist you in your search. The courts are kinder to men who work.

to change and I can't force her to; however, I can become smarter and document incidents with my son. I can take the issue to court and allow justice to eventually be served, keeping in mind that child custody cases are sometimes more of a marathon than a sprint. We can't control the selfish antics that our kids mother's often use. We can only control our actions.

If you have been in and out of court for child support, you know first hand how irritating it can be. I have been in court for the last five years. I often wonder, *If I am taking care of my child, why do I need to be taken to court?* Then I get dressed and go because I'm scheduled to be there.

Some women use the court system to get revenge on a man or just to make his life miserable. If you are dealing with a woman doing this for no reason, knowing that you are taking care of your child or children, she is wrong. But brothers, we can't let this discourage us. Stop lying down. Stand up and show up!

I'm taking responsibility for my actions. My son is my responsibility. Yes, his mom comes off spiteful and doesn't act mature most of the time, but it's still my responsibility.

Getting over Your Baby's Mama

If your kid's mother is seeing another man, so be it. As long as he is not harming your child, it's none of your business. You can't tell her who to date and who not to date. Don't hate on her because she has a new man in her life.

When you call and she doesn't answer, leaving one voicemail works just fine. Calling thirteen times is called stalking or being obsessive compulsive. Is that how you want your child to behave in their adult life? Bad habits carry over from one generation to the next. It's not the end of the world that she has moved on. Everyone hurts over someone or something at some point in life. You'll heal because time consistently proves to have a way of healing wounds.

Put an end to the control issues. It's not normal to sit in the bushes waiting to see who your child's mother is bringing back to her apartment for dinner. You date every woman in the city, but you don't want her seeing anyone. Stop causing drama. It's over. You are not with her anymore. She asked you to move on years ago. It hurts, but you need to let it go and take care of the kids.

NO MORE EXCUSES: Black Men Stand Up!

Drama is unhealthy for the children and equally unhealthy for the parents. Every time you argue in front of that child, you are damaging his or her self-esteem and you are teaching them that unresolved animosity is acceptable. Find a way to get along even if you have to bring in a mediator to help sort out unresolved conflict.

Men, we have to stand strong no matter what the circumstances. We have to show some self-control and self-restraint. Even if she is acting crazy, taking your money, dragging you in and out of court, dating all kinds of guys around your children, talking bad about you around your kids, it's still our responsibility to be parents to our kids so disregard her and stay focused on your children.

CHAPTER 11

Taking Care of Another Man's Child

Single parent homes account for most of our population. Divorces, second and third marriages are common place in black communities. A majority of our young black men are being raised by single mothers. Either they see their father very little or not at all. I was raised the same way. My mom was my mother and my father. My real father never came around for visitation or anything else. I didn't even know he existed until a few years ago. He has been dead for over ten years.

Majority of our young black men are being raised by single women along with the weak brothers who call themselves boyfriends or husbands, but really don't understand that taking proper care of the woman in their lives means to also take care of her kids.

My step-father was one of those weak brothers who mistreated me because I wasn't his biological son. He married my mom, but wanted nothing to do with me. He would constantly do things behind my mom's back to degrade me. Anytime something went wrong at the house, I was blamed for it. One time I got in a car wreck when I was about sixteen years old. I broke the windshield with my head from the force of the accident. His concern wasn't about my health or well-being, only the car and its damage. My mom said something to him about his obvious lack of concern and he became more upset.

My stepfather never got the concept of raising another man's child. He wanted my mom without the kids and he let it be known in his actions. He never took me to any games or encouraged me when I played. When I was in high school, he never attended my games. Most men would have been proud to have a son that excelled in school, excelled in sports and was equally outgoing and charismatic, but he wasn't. Instead of encouraging my strengths, he always focused on my flaws.

I watched this same loser who would constantly put me down walk over my mom. I even stepped in to rescue her on one occasion when I was eleven years old, only to be punched in my face. I lost all respect for him. My jaw was swollen for days but I would protect my mom again if I had to. I bet he didn't challenge those guys he was in prison with.

Instead of being a good husband to my mother and a role model for me, he hung out in the streets and did drugs with his friends. This man did not pay the bills like real men should, but he did stay out all night and come home the next day being verbally abusive to my mom like she was the one who stayed out all night.

When I was about to go pro in football, all of a sudden, I became his son. He would tell his friends, "My son is about to go to the NFL." Before then, he would never even talk to me nor mention me to other people.

Brothers, if you meet a sister with kids and you decide to hook up with her, you are hooking up with her kids too. It's a package deal. If she has three kids and you marry her, you have three kids as well. You cannot have the woman without the children. If the fathers of these kids aren't around, you should take the responsibility and raise the children yourself. You may feel it's not your responsibility, but it is. When you say "I do," it's your responsibility from that point on.

There is nothing wrong with raising another man's child. We all belong to God. Our children belong to God, so we are already raising someone else's children. You knew that sister had kids when you met her, so step up to the plate or leave her alone. Don't start mistreating her children because they aren't yours.

Shaquille O'Neal's stepfather took Shaq in when he was a baby. He raised Shaq like he was his own son. Since he was in the military, he was strict with Shaq, which Shaq later appreciated because it made him tough. Shaq talked about it exclusively in one of his interviews during half-time of one of his games. He spoke of how his step-father, Phil, would take away his basketball if he didn't behave in school and at home. He would get whippings from him if he did something wrong.

NO MORE EXCUSES: Black Men Stand Up!

Today Shaq is a multi-millionaire basketball player with four championship rings. He just recently won his fourth championship ring with the Miami Heat. The funny part about the whole thing is Shaq's biological father was never apart of his life when he was growing up, but as soon as Shaq went pro, his real dad, along with his grandmother, tried to come forward to reconnect with him.

It appeared that they only came around because he was rich and famous with a lot of money in the bank. His father and grandmother went on a talk show in hopes of getting Shaq to come back into their lives, but they failed to get his sympathy or attention. His father's side of the family wanted a relationship with him now. The news media made a big deal of it. Shaq ignored their request and said they would not get a cent of his money and they didn't. Most people would agree that if he wasn't in his life up to this point, why try to reap the benefits of knowing him now?

Shaq's biological father didn't help his mom raise him, but I bet he wished he had done so now. You never know what kind of blessings God will pour on you for making a difference in the life of another man's child even though they don't belong to you. Shaq's father is just another example of black men not standing up.

There are benefits to taking care of another man's child. The biggest benefit is the blessings you get from the Lord and the child after you watch him graduate from high school and college and become a successful citizen in society or you watch his grades go up because of you tutoring him.

When Shaq was growing up, his mom met a military man who was man enough to take her kids as his own when he married her. He understood that it was a package deal and look how God blessed him for doing that. Shaq refers to Phil as his dad. Phil will never have to work again because he is financially stable. Shaq recalled all the times that Phil would step to the plate during hard times and showed him tough love. Phil's tough love made him a disciplined athlete and strong man as well.

What do you think Joseph thought when Mary became pregnant with Jesus even though she never had an intimate encounter with him? In the bible, *Matthew 1:18-25* states:

18 This is how the birth of Jesus Christ came about: His mother Mary was pledged to be married to Joseph, but before they came together, she was found to be with child through the Holy Spirit.

19 Because Joseph her husband was a righteous man and did not want to expose her to public disgrace, he had in mind to divorce her quietly.

20 But after he had considered this, an angel of the Lord appeared to him in a dream and said, "Joseph son of David, do not be afraid to take Mary home as your wife, because what is conceived in her is from the Holy Spirit.

21 She will give birth to a son, and you are to give him the name Jesus, [a]because he will save his people from their sins."

22 All this took place to fulfill what the Lord had said through the prophet:

23 "The virgin will be with child and will give birth to a son, and they will call him Immanuel" [b]—which means, "God with us."

24 When Joseph woke up, he did what the angel of the Lord had commanded him and took Mary home as his wife.

25 But he had no union with her until she gave birth to a son. And he gave him the name Jesus.

Joseph's wife was pregnant with God's child and Joseph still called him his child. Joseph knew that Mary was not pregnant by him, but still took Jesus in and cared for him. As men, we must take the same approach as Joseph. He knew he didn't impregnate Mary, but he raised Jesus. Many women will have kids when you meet them, but that shouldn't make the children unlovable. There are some good women out there whose kids need attention, respect and care.

Your Responsibility

Whether you are married to a woman who has kids by someone else, coach kids in football, basketball or track, teach and mentor, as men we must accept the role of raising someone else's child. We cannot take lightly our involvement with the children we encounter because of our jobs or community involvement, especially if their fathers are not in their lives. Your influence in their lives could make the difference in their emotional and spiritual well-being.

There are many reasons why you may find yourself in the position to help take care of a child. The father could have passed away. If that is the case, the child is likely looking for father figure. Step into that role. Maybe the child's parents divorced and the father does not live in the city or isn't involved with the child. The child's father may be no where to be found or is incarcerated. At any rate, step in and lend an ear, advice, and/or financial assistance, especially for a kid who is reaching for help.

Your Role in Raising Another Man's Child

1. **To provide.** Make sure the child has food, shelter, clothes, etc.

2. **To protect.** The child should feel safe. You can't be in his home, but the child should feel safe sharing with you his problems, concerns and fears.

3. **To pray.** The child should see you praying, worshipping God. You should also keep the child in prayer.

Look at all the people it took to raise you. You had mentors, youth counselors, coaches, teachers, community leaders, etc. It's like that saying, "It takes a village to raise a child." Men we have to stand together if we want to save our young brothers. Even though I know the children don't belong to me, I'm going to do the best that I can for them. There are so many men and women out there already doing this, but we need more people stepping to the plate.

Our young men are lost in the storm. Some of them haven't been raised by real men. That's why they act the way they do. When you see one of these kids, realize that it is your responsibility to reach out and help. Take the time to talk to him about what's going on in his life. Ask him about his grades. Let him know you are there for him no matter what.

Consequences of
Not Raising Another Man's Child

1. If you don't raise them, the streets will. We are losing too many of our young men to drugs and gang violence.

2. Lack of education, which leads to lack of knowledge, which leads to lack of employment, which leads to poverty and crime.

3. We will have a generation of young boys who will grow up thinking that no one cared enough to get involved. Majority of them will become resentful and neglect the generation to follow, and the painful cycle will continue.

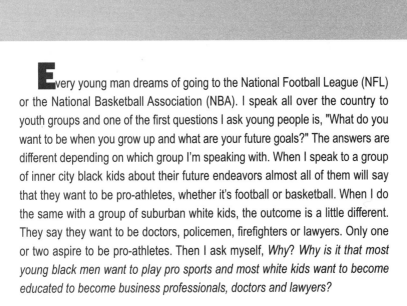

CHAPTER 12

NFL
(Not For Long)

Every young man dreams of going to the National Football League (NFL) or the National Basketball Association (NBA). I speak all over the country to youth groups and one of the first questions I ask young people is, "What do you want to be when you grow up and what are your future goals?" The answers are different depending on which group I'm speaking with. When I speak to a group of inner city black kids about their future endeavors almost all of them will say that they want to be pro-athletes, whether it's football or basketball. When I do the same with a group of suburban white kids, the outcome is a little different. They say they want to be doctors, policemen, firefighters or lawyers. Only one or two aspire to be pro-athletes. Then I ask myself, *Why*? *Why is it that most young black men want to play pro sports and most white kids want to become educated to become business professionals, doctors and lawyers?*

Desiring The Fast Road to Riches

I was guilty of it too. I can't lie. Growing up in the hood with very little, sports were all I knew. Athletes had it made with the money, the women and the power. I was one of those young black boys that used to eat, sleep and drink football. When I was growing up, we played football every day before and after school.

We all dreamed of playing in the pros, trying to find the easiest track to financial freedom. At least, it was the fastest way in our minds. Other than selling drugs, we were unaware of any other way. We went to class and studied, but sports consumed us. We would call ourselves some of the ex-greats like Tony Dorsett, Walter Payton, "Mean" Joe Greene or Jerry Rice.

Young black men in today's society share the same dream, especially when they learn about the salaries that superstars get when they sign on with teams. Professional ball players' salaries are public knowledge. Everyone knows what they make. Just turn to Sports Center if you want to hear whose making the most money and for how long. This is what captures our young peoples' attention. They want to be the next LeBron James.

James came straight out of high school and signed a $100 million contract to play with the Cleveland Cavaliers, along with a $90 million contract with NIKE™ and a $50 million contract with Sprite™. I don't know LeBron, but I do watch Sports Center. Now that LeBron made a quick, seemingly effortless financial come up, there are thousands of other young men who think they can do it as well. Unfortunately, out of all of those thousands, one may make it if he's lucky.

Are You Focused on School or the Money?

With the aspiration of making that kind of money, young men are not focusing on school. They want to get out of school and into the pros as quickly as possible. They are aware of the possibility of leaving college early and most only want to do just enough to maintain minimum requirements to play sports. The law was just changed in basketball last year, stating that players had to complete at least one year of college before entering the NBA Draft and it kept Greg Oden out for a year, but he still went number one in the draft after having a successful year at Ohio State. In the NFL, players can't leave school until they complete at least two years of college.

This doesn't apply to all of our young men though. Some of them actually go to school and take their education seriously. As they get older, the numbers tend to go down a little when asked about playing pro-ball. They realize that they are more likely to go pro in something other than sports.

As I speak to older groups of young men, some of them realize that there is a better chance that they will become business professionals or corporate executives instead of professional ball players. It has been researched and proven that less than one percent of college athletes will play professional football and the percentage is even lower for basketball players. Despite what the statistics state, our young men chase the dream day after day with no back up plan and no thought of what to do if sports don't work out. What if you get hurt? What if no one drafts or signs you? What is your alternate plan of action?

NFL stands for Not for Long. Even if you make it in the pros, it probably won't be for long. At least that's what statistics say. There is nothing wrong with leaning on your academic abilities as much as your athletic abilities. I know I'm thankful that I took school seriously.

Life After Sports: Are You Prepared?

Doctors and lawyers are role models too. Teachers and construction workers are role models also. Young brothers I'm not trying to burst your bubble, but the likelihood of you making it to the NFL or the NBA is like jumping out of an airplane trying to hit a target with no parachute. There are thousands and thousands of colleges all over the country and most of these colleges have football and basketball teams and as I mentioned earlier, less than one percent of these athletes will make it to the pros.

I'm just stating the facts. No one is telling you to give up on your dream. I just want to encourage you to have a back up plan just in case you don't make it, or you make it and your career is cut short due to injury or being cut from the team. I'm not speaking about what I think, I'm speaking about what I know. I know the devastation of an interrupted dream because I didn't expect to be cut by the Minnesota Vikings. I was planning on playing professional football for at least ten years, but it didn't happen that way. I had an injured knee in camp, but I continued to work hard to make the team. After I was cut from Minnesota, I continued to work out, but it took my knee over two years to heal completely. I had to fall back on my education sooner than I expected, but was thankful I had it because I really needed it.

No one talked to me about life after sports because all of my family and friends were expecting me to make the team and help them out of poverty. No one expected me to get cut. I didn't expect me to be cut.

The average life of an NFL ball player is three to four years. If you go pro when you are 21 years old, statistics say your career will be over by the time you are 24 or 25 if not before then. Nonetheless many young brothers go to school to focus on sports rather than to get their college degree.

Even when you get done with sports, you have to plan for your future. You are going to need a job one day, so your education is important. Our economy is getting worse. The job market is very competitive and if you don't have your education, you will be left behind. Even if you have your education, a good job is not promised to you. So planning beyond a professional athletic career is essential.

Steps to Getting Prepared for Life after Sports

1. Have a back up plan in case sports don't work out for you.

2. Take school seriously and get your education.

3. Practice and play every down like it's your last, but when it's over, let it go and move on.

4. Find ways to stay competitive even in your profession.

5. Speak to younger kids about your experiences (It's very rewarding).

6. Talk to someone who has been through it before. It's very helpful in coping with the range of emotions you may experience, including disappointments, regrets, depression, and loss of esteem.

Many pro athletes spend huge sums of their money in the first year or two trying to buy material possessions to impress others. They often get caught up in purchasing cars and jewelry while few save or invest for the future, assuming that their careers will last forever. The average NFL player made $250,000 a year in 1996 and uncle sam takes 40% of that off the top. By the time you buy a house, a few cars, and help out struggling family members, that money is all but gone.

Even with such a lucrative salary, an ex-pro athlete can't afford to pay for everyone's dinner anymore or buy expensive cars that cost more than most houses because they will run out of money. They can't fly all over the country dating girls in every city unless they had invested and saved their money to live that kind of lifestyle. If you are fortunate enough to make a professional sports team, put your money up and think about your life after sports. You will still have a lot of living to do and retiring early and adequately compensated may happen for you, but it's not likely for the average individual.

Don't Walk Away Without Your Degree

College tuition is going up every year while some athletes get scholarships to cover all of those expenses, but refuse to take advantage of it. They go to school, but don't go to class and when graduation comes around they are left off the roster. Others don't apply themselves in class or flunk out of school, cheating themselves.

With a scholarship, your college degree is promised to you if you take it seriously, however a professional career in athletics is not. College is your time to mature into a young man. You have four to five years to have fun and work toward your degree. If you are chosen to go pro, that's a bonus.

It's a blessing to go to school on scholarship, but I understand that sometimes it seems like it's not enough, especially if your parents are too poor to send you spending money. The scholarship doesn't take care of clothes, food late at night, shoes, coats for the winter and miscellaneous items. I remember getting hungry late at night. It's tough being away from the world, practicing all the time. Other students can do what they want to do, but college athletes are obligated to a schedule most of the time.

Athletes who aren't appreciative of their scholarship should talk to someone who had student loans to pay after graduating. I had many friends that were struggling just to eat from day to day. They didn't have scholarships and had to survive the best way they could, but they were determined to make it so they endured those challenges and stayed in school. That's why I don't understand why brothers don't take full advantage of the opportunities in front of them. An athletic scholarship provides free meals, a free place to lay your head and paid tuition. In return, if you do what is asked of you, you will keep your scholarship.

It's almost like they own you for the four to five years you are there. You get up when they tell you. You go places when they tell you. You eat when they tell you. You sleep when they tell you. If you are late to dinner, you don't eat because the café closes up. It's not as easy as it looks. Getting up at 5 a.m. in the morning to work out, going to practice even when you don't feel like it, going to study hall, not being able to party on the weekends like your peers is not always fun. But, if you have an athletic scholarship, I still believe it's worth the trade off.

If you are blessed to get a scholarship, you should appreciate it, especially if your families have fought hard to take care of you and push you through school. If you don't have any student loans to pay back after graduation, you are blessed. I feel that I am. I'm sure your family would not complain.

When I played football at Western Kentucky, I came in with 30 freshman football players. From that time until I graduated five years later only four of my teammates who came in with me graduated on that day. Although some of my teammates transferred to other schools, many of them dropped out, even though they were receiving a free education.

Football players take longer to develop then basketball players. Basketball players are tall and some of them are ready to go to the pros straight from high school because their bodies don't have to be developed like football players. When I graduated from high school, I was only 185 pounds. By the time I graduated from college, I was 235 pounds. This was a result of our strenuous weight training programs, which included getting our bodies prepared for long hard hitting practices and games endured over a season.

High School football was a cake walk compared to college football. The players look totally different in college. They are much bigger, stronger and faster because they are the best players from every high school across the country. As good as they are, many of these guys aren't ready for the next level; but think they are. That's why there is a rule that college football players cannot leave school until after their sophomore year.

NO MORE EXCUSES: Black Men Stand Up!

One college player, decided to challenge the law ruling freshman ineligible for the NFL draft. He was a star athlete in high school with high hopes when he signed with Ohio State University to play football. He had a great freshman year breaking almost all of the freshman records. Ohio State beat the Miami Hurricanes for the National Championship that year. The player was the star freshman running back on that winning team, so he felt he was ready for the next level. He didn't have a great game, but he did score a touchdown against the Miami Hurricanes, which was tough to do that year. He thought he was ready to go to the pros, but was told he didn't have enough experience yet.

Instead of being patient and developing his skills as a good football player, he listened to those who told him he was better than what he was. Then he decided to challenge a long standing rule with the NCAA and entered the NFL draft as a freshman. His leaving school early became nationwide news. No one had ever tried to challenge this rule.

The NFL was furious at his actions after he went public with his plans to challenge this rule by taking it to court. The court case went on for several weeks, but he eventually lost against the NFL. Since he had signed with an agent, he was ineligible to go back to Ohio State to play that year.

He shouldn't have left in the first place because although he wanted to go back to school, it was too late. During that year, he appeared in the media on several occasions at Ohio State games signing autographs, etc. He didn't appear as committed as other players. He seemed more concerned with his media coverage. He wasn't working out and was gaining weight. It's hard to stay disciplined when people telling you that you are better than what you really are and you don't have a set schedule or coach breathing down your back, keeping you on track.

Since he had sat out a year, he needed to be disciplined enough to work out on his own and stay in shape. Although he did not, he was still invited to the NFL Combine in Indianapolis. The NFL Combine brings in the best football players from all over the country to test them in several areas including their agilities, the 40 meter dash, vertical jump, running routes and catching passes. Hundreds of NFL scouts are there observing. At the combine he was not in the best shape and it showed. He had gained close to twenty pounds since his last college game and that's too much for a running back.

He ran the 40 meter dash in 4.8 seconds, which is extremely slow for an NFL running back. NFL backs should run a 4.5 or better to be respected. Four point six seconds is considered high by most NFL scouts. He was an embarrassment to the combine, but he was still drafted in the third round by the Denver Broncos. Denver Coach, Mike Shanahan, decided to take a chance on him.

Most players drafted in the third round were almost assured a roster spot on the team. You would have to mess up really bad to be cut. However, this guy showed up for camp the same way he showed up for the NFL Combine, out of shape and not mentally prepared for the task before him. His work ethic was so poor in Broncos camp that he was cut from the team. Because the coach had talked of how lazy he was, no other team wanted to sign him. To make matters worse for him, when he first signed with the Broncos, he didn't accept his signing bonus because he was encouraged to put the money into his incentives package so he could receive more money later in his contract. The incentives package included extra money he would receive if he scored so many touchdowns or gained so many yards and played in so many games. That was a very bad decision on his part. Whoever advised him to pass up his signing bonus gave him poor advice. He passed up over $300,000 that he would have received just for signing his name on the contract. He didn't touch a dime of that money.

What he didn't understand was that NFL contracts are not guaranteed. If you get cut, the contract is null and void and you are owed nothing, unless you get injured before you get cut. If you are injured while playing, the NFL owes you at least until you heal up. When he was cut from the Broncos, he walked away with nothing. He did have minor injuries during football camp, but was cut during training camp after his injuries had healed up. The head coach of the Denver Broncos said he had made a mistake in drafting him so high in the draft, and although he had taken a chance on him, he wasn't losing anything since he turned down his signing bonus.

Remember, he had dropped out of college to go pro, so he had no back up plan. He had embarrassed himself by being cut as a third round draft pick. He had left the Denver Broncos the same way he came in, with no money.

He returned back to Ohio State reportedly owing several people money because they thought he would pay them back after the NFL paid him. That's what the agents and others do when they think you are going to make it big, they give you cash advances. Some hopefuls get money up front from everyone they know who has it and sometimes money comes in from people who want their money back right away. He was like most young football players. When he found out he was about to be drafted, he started buying up things he couldn't afford and spent money he didn't have yet. Since he had no money, instead of getting a job, he decided to rob some Ohio State students for their cell phone and wallets just days before he was supposed to sign with the World Football League, which is a developmental league for the NFL, where he could work on skills and possibly go back to the NFL.

This is how quick it can all go wrong. He had won a national championship with Ohio State as a freshman, than he had been on ESPN everyday for challenging the NFL. Everyone knew him and then he decided to throw his life away by robbing innocent students and ended up in jail. Before he could go to trial for this case, he was found drunk on the side of the road with a bullet proof vest on and several loaded weapons in his car. He was thrown in jail, without bail. After a short trial, he was sentenced to seven years in prison. No one really knew the full story of where he was going with all of those guns, but it couldn't have been anywhere positive.

This is what no back up plan can lead to. He had moved too quickly and put all of his eggs in one basket and thought the NFL would be his final destination. There are several NFL Hall of Fame running backs like Barry Sanders, Marcus Allen, Walter Payton and Terrell Davis and none of them left school after their freshman year. He could have had a free college education instead of going to jail if he would have just waited before leaving school early. If you are ever in this situation, think about the importance of a backup plan. Get your education. Don't go to school just to play sports.

There were so many of my college teammates who dropped out of college to work out for NFL teams without getting their college degrees. Now they are barely making ends meet. There were very few who made it into camps, but out of those who actually made it to camp only one or two made someone's roster for maybe one or two seasons, if that.

My college roommate Eddie Godfrey was drafted by the Tampa Bay Buccaneers my sophomore year of college. He was a kick returner and Defensive Back at WKU. He was lightning quick and very strong for his size. He made it all the way to the last cuts with Tampa Bay but got cut. My friend Bill Miller was drafted by the Detroit Lions when he came out of Illinois State. He made it all the way to the last cuts and got released from the team also. The thing I admire about both of these guys was their course of action. When plan A didn't work out, both of them had back up plans. They didn't count on football to take them through life. We all took a chance of making someone's roster and didn't make the final cut, but we all have our college degrees and are doing well.

Just because you get your degree, doesn't mean you won't struggle in life. There are thousands of college graduates looking for jobs right now. Everyone struggles at some point in their lives. We had our ups and downs, but we are still here and doing well.

Eddie has his own limousine business in Florida, while Bill is one of the top sales reps at his company in Detroit. I'm also doing well in pharmaceutical sales, where I have won numerous awards. We wouldn't be where we are today without our education. Young brother if you must chase after that ball, get your education in the process.

Make it a priority to finish school no matter what. Even if you make it to the NFL or NBA draft, finish school. There are far too many of us who can't read or write and count on our athletic ability to carry us through life. What are you going to do if you blow out a knee or break your ankle? What is your back up plan? Do you think you will play forever? The answer is no.

Getting your education is a plus. It will work out in your favor in the long run whether you make someone's roster or not. My education can never be taken away from me. It's the reason I am who I am today. I still have dreams and aspirations that I haven't fulfilled yet, but I'm on my way. One of them was writing this book. There is nothing wrong with dreaming, but if you aren't putting it into motion you are wasting your time. We need to face the facts about pro sports. It's tough getting in and close to 96% of pro athletes need jobs after their careers are over.

These days you can't count on one thing to help you make it through life. Try your hands at several things and then you will see what you are good at. Don't put all of your eggs in one basket with pro sports. There is a commercial out that shows a bunch of college athletes both male and female. It says, "The NCAA is full of athletes and over 99% of them will go pro in something other than sports." That statement is so true. Every single person I played football with in college is done with sports. I don't know of anyone still playing at this point. Every one has moved on to their life's work.

Some of us took school seriously. Others decided to skip class and play around. They decided that partying was their favorite class and left school without their education, even though it was free to them. Many young men dream of becoming the next LeBron James. LeBron James was an honor roll student in high school, which means that he went to class and studied to make his grades. Don't fool yourself, thinking you are going to make it on your talent alone. As soon as the lights go out it's over.

Trying to make it on athletic ability alone is a big risk. The rules are set up today that if your grades are too low, you won't receive your athletic scholarship and you will be put on probation. The NCAA makes you sit out a year and if you don't get your grades up, you lose your scholarship and go home. I agree with this rule because prior to it too many of our young men were being set up for failure. This rule challenges athletes to take school seriously.

A Long Road to a Short Stay

I had aspirations and dreams just like millions of other young men all over the country of playing in the NFL. I stayed in school on my full scholarship and utilized my resources. Western Kentucky used my legs to run that football and the 100m and 200m dashes in track and I used them to get a free education. I was not going to leave that school without my college degree. It meant too much to me, but I still planned to play ten years in the NFL.

I started playing organized football at an early age at Wheelers Boys Club when I was nine years old. As much as I loved football, I was scared to get hit the first time I put on a uniform. Wheelers Boys Club was one of the most competitive leagues in the city at the time and several players went on to play at Division I colleges and in the NFL.

I didn't start playing for my school until sixth grade. Even though I knew I was good enough to play, from sixth grade through eleventh grade I barely saw the field. I was on the team, but was on the side lines watching. I would go in when we were winning by a large margin. My coaches didn't believe in me, so I didn't get to play. No one I played with played every year from sixth grade through twelfth grade like I had. It was painful watching from the sideline when I knew I was good enough to be on the field. I practiced day after day and year after year.

People often ask me why I never quit the team since I never got a chance to play. Something in me wouldn't let me quit. I have never been a quitter. I felt that I would get my chance one day and I was going to be ready for it. I was determined to get my shot on the field even though it didn't look good for me. I had coaches telling me that I should move on to something else, that football wasn't for me, but I never gave up on my dream and didn't listen to them.

As time went on, I started to get discouraged. It was tough remaining committed but I kept trying. I wanted to play bad, so I stayed on that team even though I was on the bench, not knowing it would take six years of riding the bench before I caught a break. There was a new head coach hired at my high school that would give me that shot. It was my senior year of high school, Coach Dave Enright, our new football coach, took a chance on me and started me at running back.

He didn't regret it. During the first game I ever touched the ball, I was on my way to one of many 100 yard rushing games, when we were rained out. During the course of that season, I compiled over 1600 yards receiving and rushing. Unlike former coaches at my high school who had no confidence in me, this new coach saw something in me. He saw the same thing that I had seen in myself all these years. It had been frustrating sitting on the bench, but it finally paid off. My teammates and other coaches began to recognize my talent and often wondered why I had been on the bench for so long.

I was told, "I didn't know you could run like that" or "I didn't know you had good hands like that." I ran an 80-yard touchdown and caught a 90-yard touchdown in the same game.

My teammates voted me MVP (Most Valuable Player) at our award's banquet. I tell young people all the time that you have to believe in yourself. I waited all those years to play and when I finally got my chance, I was voted the best player on my team. You don't just wake up and get the MVP. I had those skills all along.

My teammates didn't know that even though I was riding the bench, I stayed in shape and I kept working on my skills when they weren't around. I would run some nights until I threw up my food. My legs would be in so much pain. My chest would hurt from lifting weights.

Several colleges wanted to sign me. I signed with Western Kentucky University (WKU). I was also given a scholarship and the okay to play both football and run track. My high school coach encouraged me to go there. That was one of the best decisions I made.

Even though I only started one year in high school, I started at running back four years for Western Kentucky and I ran track. It was funny because I had to start over again in college. When I walked on that campus, I didn't know anyone, but I was determined to succeed. I had waited all those years in high school to play and then I had to prove myself all over again. This time I got playing time a lot sooner. I got my shot during my red shirt freshman year and never looked back. During my junior year at WKU our offense was ranked number two in the country in Division I-AA football. It was no surprise my senior year, when our offense was ranked number one in the nation in rushing offense. I was a key part of that offense.

During my senior year of college I was drawing looks from the NFL, but I remembered what I had promised my mom, my coach and myself. I had promised not to leave there without my degree, which I received on May 8th, 1994. It was Mother's Day and I presented my mom with my Bachelor of Science Degree as her Mother's Day gift.

After graduation, I felt that I was one step closer to my dream of playing in the NFL. I had over 1300 all-purpose yards my senior year at Western Kentucky and was having talks with agents and NFL scouts. I signed with an agent out of Los Angeles. On draft day I was in Atlanta, Georgia. I watched the whole draft to find that my name wasn't called. The draft had been cut from thirteen rounds to seven by the time I graduated from college. I was devastated because my agent said I was projected to go somewhere between rounds five and seven. It was one of the most disappointing days of my life.

I had worked for so long to play in the National Football League and no one had drafted me. After going to Colts camp, Raiders camp, and Rams camp, I finally signed with the Minnesota Vikings later that next year. Right before I was leaving for camp, my best friend, Larry Shotwell, was found dead in the trunk of someone's car. Earlier that summer, I lost another close friend, Tye "Binky" Smith in a car accident, to make matters worse my mom was extremely sick.

It seemed like everything I had worked for was falling apart. Whatever could go wrong that summer, went wrong. I tried to stay focused when I went to Minnesota for camp, but continued to have nightmares about the deaths of my friends. I focused as much as I could and seemed to be doing well in camp despite what I had been going through. I was doing well in practice and was learning the system. I just knew I had made the team. When they called my name to go see the coach during the last cuts, I was shocked. I didn't understand why I had come that far for things to just fall apart. I had hurt my knee also. It ended up taking my knee over two years to heal. After getting cut, I came back home in a deep depression. I got so close, but didn't make the team. I felt that part of the blame was my mental state. I had gone through so much in such a short period of time.

I continued to rehab my knee and worked out as much as I could. I received a call from the Green Bay Packers requesting to work me out. I bench pressed 225 Pounds 32 times, but my knee was not ready for the agility drills, catching passes and the 40 meter dash. I would usually run as fast as 4.4 seconds or lower in the 40 meter dash, but during those work outs I ran a 4.5 and 4.6, which hurt my chances of getting into camp.

I went to the World Football League with the London Monarchs briefly, but wasn't motivated to play outside of the NFL. I knew there was a chance for me to make someone's roster. I felt that all the other running backs were not better than me. I was healthy and strong prior to my knee injury.

The Pittsburgh Steelers called me for a private work out. I had always liked the Steelers from my childhood memories of Terry Bradshaw, "Mean" Joe Greene and Franco Harris. They flew me out there for the work out. When I walked into the locker room I admired the four Super Bowl Trophies standing in a case right by the Steelers front office with pictures of Terry Bradshaw, Franco Harris and Lynn Swan. That day was one of the coldest days of the year in Pittsburgh. I believe the wind chill was well below zero. The football field was also the baseball field for the Pittsburgh Pirates. It also rained really bad the night before. I went outside to begin my warm ups, but I couldn't warm my body up. It was so cold outside. I ran a 4.5 seconds and 4.6 seconds 40 meter dash and the scout told me, "I thought you were faster than that." I knew I was faster than that also, but the NFL is all about timing and they don't have time to wait for your knee to heal because thousands of others are waiting around to take your turn. My knee had only been healed for a few days before the Steelers called me to come out there to work out.

I was deeply disappointed that I didn't make anyone's roster. Many of my friends and family members were hurt as well. Everyone was counting on me to go pro and play several years in the NFL. I felt like I had let my whole family down.

After feeling sorry for myself for sometime, I realized that I did have a college degree. I did have a backup plan. Now I needed to put it into motion. I knew that I had a gift from God of speaking and ministering to youth, so I took a job at the Indianapolis Urban League working with kids. After one year there, I took a job teaching Industrial Technology at Arlington High School and I also coached the track team. I left Arlington High School to become the Lead Program Manager with the Indianapolis Housing Agency where I stayed for six years. I then became a Professional Sales Rep with GlaxoSmithKline. I am currently a Specialty Rep with Teva Specialty Pharmaceuticals.

My life wasn't over. It had just begun. Many of our young men have the same dreams that I had. I was thankful to play in the National Football League, as brief as it was. I played with and against some of the best players in the world. When I look back at how I rode the bench all those years in grade school and part of high school and how I made it to the NFL, I know I accomplished something great. I know that I made it. I also beat the odds of young athletes not taking school seriously by receiving my degree.

Jerry Rice played twenty two years in the NFL and Emmitt Smith played fifteen years before retiring, but those are rare instances. There are so many Ex-NFL ball players who are without an education, without a job and barely making it. They don't have money to pay their bills because they blew it on lavish lifestyles.

Nothing Wrong With Dreaming

It's okay to go after the dream of playing in the NFL or NBA, but remember to have a back up plan. Your career may last twenty years, twenty days or twenty seconds. Many of you will never make it into an NFL or NBA camp. It's so difficult just to make it to that point and even if you do, you may or may not last. There is so much competition and everyone feels like they deserve to be there.

If you can make it into a NFL or NBA camp and even make the team, that's great. Just know that your career will be over one day and you will spend a majority of your life in the workforce unless you save or invest into the right things. More times than not, your career will be over before you reach your 26th birthday. Think ahead. Are you really going to retire at 26? Probably not.

I'm thankful for the experience even though it was short. That experience has helped me to touch the lives of others, including kids in public schools, public housing and other youth groups. I feel like God took me through my experiences for a reason. Colleges use our athletes like cattle to play sports, so athletes need to be smart enough to use colleges and universities to pay for their education, which can take you further than most anything you ever do in life including athletics. No matter how good you run the football or dunk the basketball, there will come a time when you play in your last game. As time goes on, as you keep living and getting older, your legs will eventually get old and give out on you. You will not be as fast as you once were. Your muscles will also deteriorate and you will not be as strong as you used to be, but your mind will outlast them all and your education will never leave you. No matter who you are, no one plays forever. Even Jerry Rice had to hang up his cletes after twenty-two seasons in the NFL. He made a lot of money and won several championships with the 49ers, but he too had to hang it up.

Michael Jordan is another example. He won three championships with the Bulls in the early 90's took a couple of seasons off to play baseball and then came out of retirement to win three more championships before he retired again. He was still young at the time and at the top of his game. Many say if Jordan hadn't taken two years off, he probably would have eight rings. His presence in the NBA kept a lot of superstars from getting championship rings including, Charles Barkley, Patrick Ewing, Dennis Johnson, Karl Malone and many more. Even though Jordan was a superstar on the court, as time went on his skills started to diminish. He won championships, MVP titles, scoring titles, All-Star appearances, Slam Dunk Contests and played in ten or more seasons. At one time he wasn't convinced that he was done. This was after his last championship, which was his sixth ring with the bulls. Michael retired for a few seasons and then he tried to make a comeback with the Washington Wizards.

The point is, even the great Michael Jordan had to hang it up after a while. Jordan was a rare breed. He actually went to college for two years before leaving North Carolina to join the bulls, but he went back to get his degree. Today he is a multi-millionaire and owns part of the NBA Charlotte Bobcats. He also has his own shoe and clothing line and he's worth over 200 million dollars.

If you believe in yourself, keep working toward your dream. There is a price to pay to be the best. If you have aspirations of being a pro ball player, go after it with everything you have. Give it your best shot. Work out like your life depended on it. You may be one of the lucky few, but if it doesn't work out for you after having given it your best shot, have an education to fall back on.

Know When It's Time to Walk Away

In sports, you always have that group of guys who try out for pro teams and never give it up. Every time you speak with them, they are telling you about one of their workouts they had the week before or one that is about to take place. Some of them are well into their 30's and early 40's and have never played organized football, but talk about trying out for different NFL teams. Others never smelled a pro camp, but every time you speak with them, they are about to try out for another team. Brother, let it go. If you have tried out for over ten years and haven't made a team yet, chances are you will never make a team. Brothers, when it's over, it's over. Stop telling people you are trying out next year for the Colts. Stop telling girls your agent is working on it, because you don't have an agent.

A 30 year-old who never played college ball anywhere and continues to try out every time a new camp comes to town may get lucky, but it's a long shot. Sometimes you have to just move on to whatever God has in store for you and your life. It is unlikely that a 5'5, 120 pound guy who has played semi-pro football for the last five years and didn't even start on that team, is ready for the pros. Just think about it before you decide to chase it forever. Life will pass you by if you don't watch it.

Everyone has to move on, including me. For me, it was teaching and mentoring youth when I first left the NFL. For you it may be something else. Be careful not to hold on to the dream too long and miss out on other blessings.

My hope is that you stay in school to get your degree, try out for a professional ball club and win a position on the team, but if it doesn't work out for you, your degree will carry you through life. You may play in the NBA or the NFL, but "Not For Long."

CHAPTER 13

It's God's Body
Take Care of It

Our bodies belong to God, but he gave us the tools needed to take care of them while in our possession. Nonetheless, many of us do more harm than good to our bodies on a daily basis. As a result, men are in serious danger of dying because of lack of knowledge, infrequent doctor visits, not eating right and not exercising. Obesity and disease have taken over and black men are at the top of the list of those affected. Statistics have shown that we suffer from disease much more often than any other race on the planet. Not taking care of your body shortens your life and many of us just don't realize how sick we really are.

What the Bible says about the Human Body:
2 Corinthians 5:10
For we must all appear before the judgment seat of Christ, so that each one may receive what is due for what he has done in the body, whether good or evil.

All men will be judged by God according to what he has done with his body both good or bad. God intends for each of us to live a long life, but the decision lies with each of us. It's our choice to exercise and eat right. When faced with disease and sickness we must educate ourselves about our illnesses and take it more seriously by treating our bodies with respect by adjusting our diet, making our doctor visits and following the plan he sets out for us. One step better would be to research our illnesses to become aware of all available treatment options.

What you don't know can kill you!

Black men suffer far worse in health than any other racial group in America. There are a number of reasons for this. Poor health education is the number one reason, but other reasons include abuse of drugs and alcohol, not getting enough rest, not eating right, not exercising regularly and not getting check ups twice a year by our doctors.

Black Male Health Statistics

Listed below are recent statistics regarding black men and our health issues from Health, U.S., 2003, Table 3. As alarming as they are, the numbers can be decreased with basic lifestyle changes.

- Black men live 7.1 years less than other racial groups
- Blacks have higher death rates in all of the leading causes of death
- 40% of black men die prematurely from cardiovascular disease as compared to 21% of white men
- Black men are 5 times more likely to die of HIV/AIDS
- Black men have a 60% higher diabetes-related death than whites
- Black men have 30% higher Heart Failure death
- Black men have 25% higher cancer deaths (Lung, Prostate, Colon)
- Black men with prostate cancer are 2-3 times more likely to die than whites.
- Black men have twice as many strokes as whites.
- Black men who suffer a stroke have a 95% higher death rate than whites
- Blacks are more likely to be obese and to have hypertension.
- In Black men, high blood pressure is epidemic. Severe high blood pressure leads to greater rates of stroke, heart attack, and kidney failure.
- Black men have the highest rate of prostate cancer in the world.
- 44% of black men are considered overweight
- 24% are obese
- Black men suffer more preventable oral diseases that are treatable

• Black s have a high suicide rate. It's the 3rd leading cause of death in 15 to 24 year olds

These statistics are staggering, but very true. Many of us have male family members who are suffering from one of these illnesses on this list. Many of you reading this book are on this list.

Reasons to Stay Healthy

There are a number of reasons to stay healthy including living a longer life, family, quality of life and reproduction. It has been proven that those who take care of their bodies, live longer lives. I just spoke with a gentleman not too long ago who is now 95 years old. He told me the key to long life is doing things in moderation, including exercising, eating and drinking alcohol. Living a longer life means spending more time with your family. Some of us have children that we would like to see grow up while others long to have grandchildren. Many would like to live their lives without using a wheelchair or walker. Breathing on your own and not using a machine is a blessing to most. Staying healthy improves your quality of life and makes reproduction easier. People have been known to die during child birth and some are not healthy enough to have children through natural birth. There are men not healthy enough to produce kids at all.

Why I Chose to Become Healthy

Disease runs in my family whether it's high blood pressure, kidney disease or diabetes. Both my mom and grandmother are on dialysis. My mom has been on dialysis for eighteen years. I've been an athlete my whole life and didn't think it would catch me, but because of my family history it did. I was diagnosed with hypertension ten years ago. I took medication off and on for two years, but decided one day that I didn't want to be on medication the rest of my life, so I started exercising to lose weight. I changed my diet and started eating healthier.

I had gained an extra 35 pounds when I finished playing football and I believed that extra weight was causing my blood pressure to rise. The combination of eating right and working out helped me shave 30 of those pounds and my

Ten Leading Causes of Death in Black Americans (2001)

1. **Cardiovascular Disease** including heart attack, heart disease

2. **Cancer** including lung cancer, colon cancer, prostate cancer, brain cancer

3. **Stroke** which can be caused by high blood pressure (Hypertension)

4. **Unintentional injuries** include car accidents, falling and drowning

5. **Diabetes** causes blindness, amputation of limbs and death.

6. **Homicide** includes all the black on black crime and unsolved murders. Black men are dying at an alarming rate from homicide.

7. **HIV/AIDS** is on the rise. Some people still don't take it seriously yet more and more people are being infected with this disease in our community.

blood pressure went back to normal. I kept it to myself for a while to see if my pressure would go back up. I finally decided to let my doctor know. Every time I came into get my blood pressure checked it was normal and my doctor thought I was taking medication, but I wasn't. He was shocked when I told him I wasn't taking the medicine anymore. I haven't been on any medicine since.

Ten Leading Causes of Death in Black Americans (2001) (cont.)

8. **Chronic Lower Respiratory Disease** includes lung disease and asthma. Many black men have asthma and it's not being treated, which can cause serious injury and death. There is medicine to treat the disease, but many men don't take their medication.

9. **Nephritis, Nephrotic Syndrome and Nephrosis** is kidney disease. My mom and grandmother both suffer from this. It's treated by either dialysis treatments three days a week or a kidney transplant. If it's not treated, it can cause immediate death.

10. **Septicemia** is bacteria in the blood or blood disease.

I also decreased my stress level, which was causing a lot of my blood pressure problems, so I released some of the stress by praying and meditating more. I also let go of things that I had no control over and left them in God's hands. In some cases I had to let go of people. If you are dealing with a person who is constantly stressing you out, you need to cut that person off. If it is someone you are involved with, you may want to re-evaluate that relationship. Being stressed out more than being happy is not a healthy relationship. It's not easy letting go of people who have been in your life for a short or long time, but you must think about yourself and what's best for you. I wanted to live, so I let go and I feel 100% better.

Besides meditating on scriptures and positive affirmations that address your problem areas, to get your mind off of stressful situations, get a hobby whether it's bowling, playing chest or playing basketball with the guys once or twice a week.

Make an effort to cut down on arguing and fussing with your significant other. Choose your battles wisely. Lastly get plenty of rest. Don't underestimate the healing power of a good nights sleep. If you are working out hard and eating right and not getting proper rest, you are defeating the purpose. While sleeping, your body rejuvenates and your mind becomes revived. All of these things work together.

How to turn it around

The words that come out of your mouth need to reflect positive change because the tongue is very powerful. Whatever you speak is bound to happen. I hear people say, "I can eat what I want to eat and it's not going to hurt me." That statement is not reality based. What you eat can not only hurt you, it can kill you if you abuse it. Instead of saying, "I want to get healthy," say, "I'm *going* to get healthy starting now." It's also good to set attainable goals for yourself. Many of us want to lose weight, but we set outrageous goals like losing 100 pounds in three weeks. That's not going to happen if you do it right. An attainable goal is something that is tough, but within reach like losing ten pounds in six weeks by exercising and eating right. Put a plan in place. Working out should become a part of your daily routine so find a way to fit it into your work and home life. Decide to eat healthier.

Oftentimes eating healthy is what you intend, but you don't support it with your actions. You eat healthy one day and then splurge on junk food the next day to celebrate how well you did the day before. You have to make a choice to seek out healthier ways of preparing your favorite dishes and choosing healthier items from the restaurants you frequent. You may even need to explore new places to eat. Eating healthy has to become a way of life.

Your Body is your Temporary Castle

Your body is like your house or apartment you live in. How do you keep your home? Do you have electricity and gas for your heat and cool air? Do you clean your house? Do you have water to drink and to take a shower or bath with? Your body needs the same things. Your body needs food and water for energy. It also needs to be heated and cooled. You don't stop eating to lose weight, you have to eat right. When you eat more small healthy meals during the day it increases your metabolism, which in turn burns fat and helps you lose weight. When you stop eating you don't have anything to burn off and when you just eat heavy meals one to two times a day, it's tougher to lose weight because so much food has been consumed and is just sitting there.

According to the USDA, active men typically need around 2800 calories to reach or maintain a healthy weight. However, each individual is different, so just don't take in more calories in a day than you can work off. Otherwise you're going to stay at the same weight and you won't lose a pound. If you take in more calories in a day, just make sure you have a plan to expend them by exercising or increasing you physical activity.

Chicken and fish are healthier baked instead of fried. Increase the amount of fruit and vegetables you normally eat, preferably four fruits and five vegetables a day. Don't be alarmed by this amount, you can get servings by drinking 100% fruit juice and vegetable juice. You don't have to just eat green beans every day, there are so many choices, several kinds of greens, corn, squash, broccoli, peas, carrots, zucchini, cauliflower, brussels sprouts and many others. The more variety you eat, the wider your nutritional intake. This doesn't mean that you have to give up soul food. I know your mom or your significant other's fried chicken tastes good to you, but everything that's good to you is not good for you, so eat it in moderation.

Have an open mind when it comes to eating healthier. Your meals should be made up of fruits, vegetables, grains, nuts and beans. These foods are high in complex carbohydrates, fiber, vitamins and minerals. They are low in fat and free of cholesterol. These foods should outweigh meat and dairy products. You know how we are, brothers, we love to eat meat, but to become healthier we have to cut back on the meat.

Eat foods like broccoli, carrots, cantaloupe and citrus fruits, which have antioxidants and other nutrients that help to protect against some cancers and other diseases. Avoid sugary foods, which are high in fat and calories. Keep your cholesterol intake below 300 milligrams. To decrease your cholesterol, cut down on animal fat by choosing lean meats, skinless chicken and turkey, and nonfat and low-fat dairy products. Eat less trans fats, which are in most processed foods, including frozen dinners and many fast foods. You don't know what the food has in it when you eat out. That means stop going to the drive-thru everyday and start cooking at home more often.

How do I get started?

Consult with your physician before making any lifestyle changes. Get tested with a full screen or physical including blood tests for your blood pressure, heart, cholesterol and sugar levels. Have your doctor write you out a list of things you can and cannot do. If you don't get tested, you are only hurting yourself. Some things can be caught and treated, but not if you don't show up for your appointment.

Join a gym or if there is a facility where you work or at your apartment complex, utilize it. Get a workout partner or a personal trainer to assist you if you don't know what you are doing. It's good to have someone there to encourage you. You can also walk or run in your neighborhood with family and/or friends. Research the various forms of working out until you find what works best for you.

Speak to your significant other about contributing to changing your eating habits by purchasing more fruits and vegetables instead of potato chips and sweets. I know you love fried chicken and hot sauce, but it's not in agreement with your high blood pressure. High levels of sodium causes your blood pressure to go up, so skip the salt. Check the labels on the food you purchase. Opt for items with lower saturated fat and lower sodium.

When your doctor puts you on medication, take it! The medicine can save your life. I decided to do something to get off of it, but this may not work for everyone. Even when you feel better, continue to take your medication until you discuss with your physician the proper way to titrate down and stop taking your medication. If you are attempting to lose weight, cut your carbs after 6 p.m. Carbs include potatoes, bread, rice and pasta. Eat a large breakfast, a moderate lunch and a small dinner. If you are overweight, it's time to stop living in denial and start losing it. All programs are not good ones. I believe in getting weight off the natural way by doing cardio, lifting weights and eating properly. Watch what you eat and stay disciplined.

Don't try to eat the whole roll of bread when you go out to restaurants with your family. The bread can be so good that you can't stop eating it and that will contribute to your weight issues.

Put yourself in a better position to live longer and healthier. The way you view your body will make a world of difference in how you treat it. Respect your body, properly nourish it, keep it fit, take the proper steps to heal it and in return your body will function in a way that will allow you a full, healthy, active life for years to come.

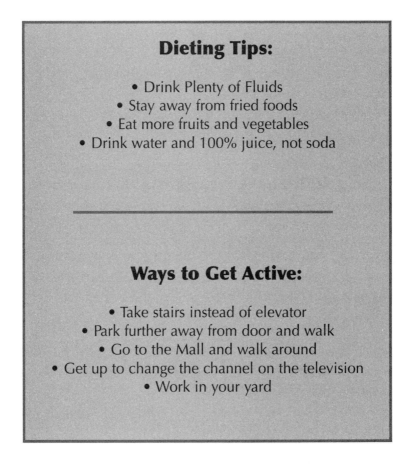

Dieting Tips:

- Drink Plenty of Fluids
- Stay away from fried foods
- Eat more fruits and vegetables
- Drink water and 100% juice, not soda

Ways to Get Active:

- Take stairs instead of elevator
- Park further away from door and walk
- Go to the Mall and walk around
- Get up to change the channel on the television
- Work in your yard

If you never worked out before. Below is a basic workout. I have been a personal trainer for over fifteen years and this is a typical workout that I offer to my clients:

Basic Workout to Get Started:
CONSULT WITH YOUR PHYSICIAN BEFORE ANY WORKING OUT!

I. Warm Up
(Walk a lap around track or ride bike for 3-5 minutes)

II. Stretch Out
Spend time in this area (15-20 seconds per stretch)

III. Cardio
Biking, Walking, Jogging, Tennis, Basketball, Stair Stepper, Treadmill, etc. (15-30 minutes – gradually increase overtime)

IV. Weights
• To Tone, stay light on the weights and do more repetitions.
• To bulk up, heavy on the weights with less repetitions. (No more than 3 days a week) Change body parts when you lift.
    a. Chest and Arms (Monday)
    b. Legs (Wednesday)
    c. Back and Shoulders (Friday)

V. Ab Work
(Usually 3 sets of 15-50 reps). This can be done daily or at least 3-4 days a week.

VI. Warm Down/Stretch

CHAPTER 14

HELP
(Healing Everyday Life's Problems)

As men we need to heal from the pain of our past. The healing process starts by admitting you have faults and recognizing when you have a problem. This is the very first step in healing from the problems that have hindered you from moving forward. If you are one of the brothers dealing with any of the issues I described in the previous chapter, it's time to step up and make a change for yourself, your family and your community.

Listed below are different resources that can help to get your life back on track. This list is by no means complete, but it is a starting place. Please refer to the books, websites or lists to help you on your journey to becoming a better man.

General Help

www.blackselfhelp.info
The Black Self-help Organization Information Website
The goal of this website is to list information about national and local organizations that are focusing on issues in the American Black community.

www.mentalhelp.net
Mental Help Net

This site is an established and highly regarded website dedicated to educating the public about mental health, wellness, and family and relationship issues and concerns. The content is provided by mental health professionals through News, articles, reviewed links, interactive tests, book reviews, self-help resources, therapist and even videos. It address topics such as ADHD, Alcohol & Substance Abuse & Addiction, Anxiety Disorders, Bipolar Disorder, Depression and many others.

Books
Reclaim Your Power!
by Terrance Dean

Reclaim... takes you through a 30 day journey that is consistent and impacting.

Healing Grace for Hurting People
by Dr. H. Norman Wright and Larry Renetzky, LMFT

Healing Grace for Hurting People is a spiritual and uplifting book for people who are hurting in any number of ways. If you are suffering or hurting from abuse, addiction, rejection or infidelity, "Healing Grace" has something for you.

"Yo, Little Brother . . .": Basic Rules of Survival for Young African-American Males
by Anthony Davis and Jeffrey Jackson

Advice to help guide the African-American male and increase his chance of success in today's society.

False Roads To Manhood
by Frank Chase, Jr.

This book will force you to deal with many of the urgent needs that every man will eventually have to face as they make their way through life.

Black Pain
by Terrie M. Williams

This book encourages us to face the truth about the issue that plunges our spirits into darkness, so that we can step into the healing light.

Anger Management

www.angermgmt.com
Leonard Ingram's AngerMgmt.com
This site offers classes, workshops, books and other resources to learning to deal with anger, domestic abuse, road rage, workplace violence, divorce, addiction, and several other areas. There is also a test on this site to measure your anger.

www.angriesout.com
If you have or know of a young child that has a tough time controlling his/her anger, this site could be helpful, although the site is for both children and adults.

Books
Playing with Anger: Teaching Coping Skills to African American Boys through Athletics and Culture
by Howard C. Stevenson
Presents unique, culturally relevant interventions that can teach coping skills to African American boys with a history of aggression.

The Anger Management Sourcebook
by Glenn R. Schiraldi and Melissa Hallmark Kerr
Shows how to empower yourself and redirect your anger into constructive behavior.

Breaking Down the Wall of Anger: Interactive Games and Activities
by Esther Williams
This innovative curriculum for dealing with anger problems in students grades five through eight, allows teachers the structure and flexibility to teach students new and creative ways to deal with their anger.

Education

www.hbcuconnect.com
The Original Historically Black College & University Community
Has scholarship information, listing of all Historically Black Colleges and Universities, blogs, forums, career center, and more.

Books
African American Student's College Guide: Your One-Stop Resource for Choosing the Right College, Getting in, and Paying the Bill
by Isaac Black
Gives inside tips on admissions, profiles of 100 top colleges, and hundreds of scholarship sources.

Beating the Odds: Raising Academically Successful African American Males
by Freeman A. Hrabowski, Kenneth I. Maton, Geoffrey L. Greif
Beating the Odds is a thoughtful examination of what parents and others who care for and about African-American males (and all children) can do to ensure that they succeed in school and in life.

Career Development

www.blackeoejournal.com
The Black Equal Opportunity Employment Journal
America's leading African-American Business and Career magazine. Every issue of the quarterly published magazine celebrates the accomplishments of African-Americans, honor, proud traditions and spotlights ways to enhance everyday life.

www.MindTools.com
Mindtools.com

This site offers advice about your career and 100 essential skill-builder articles, which are free of charge.

www.psijobfair.com
PSI

Specializes in the area of Diversity and Technical Job Fairs. Today, the PSI Professional & Technical Diversity Job Fair is the preferred Job Fair of America's premier corporations. It is the only one selected by the NAACP.

Job Training

www.doleta.gov/OA/ojt.cfm
On-the-Job-Training

Structured, supervised, on-the-job training consisting of at least 2,000 hours depending on the occupation. The apprentice is supervised during the term of the apprenticeship by a skilled craft worker(s). The supervisor reviews, evaluates and maintains records relating to the apprentice's job performance. Upon entry into the apprenticeship program, apprentice(s) are paid a progressively increasing schedule of wages.

www.dol.gov/dol/topic/training
The Department of Labor's Employment & Training Administration (ETA)

Fund job training programs to improve the employment prospects of adults, youth, and dislocated workers. These programs are delivered primarily by states through the **One-Stop Career Center System**. Training programs can vary from state to state depending on the skills that are needed to compete for jobs in the local area. All programs are aimed at boosting workers' employability and earnings.

www.acteonline.org
The Association for Career and Technical Education (ACTE)

The largest national education association dedicated to the advancement of education that prepares youth and adults for careers.

www.goodwill.org/page/guest/jobseekers/trainingprograms
Goodwill

Many local Goodwills train people for jobs in IT, healthcare, retail, food services, banking, manufacturing and more. They also help people learn office and computer skills. Local Goodwills work closely with area businesses to understand what type of jobs they have, and then tailor job training to meet the requirements of those positions.

Job Search

For full-time and all other
www.job-hunt.org
www.monster.com
www.careerbuilder.com
www.simplyhired.com

Hourly/Part-time work
www.snagajob.com - *hourly jobs*
www.collegehelpers.com – *part time jobs for college students*
http://part-time.careerbuilder.com – *part time work*
www.jobdoggy.com – *part time jobs for teens*
www.gotajob.com - *part time and summer jobs for teens and students*
www.groovejob.com - *part time jobs, teen jobs, student jobs, hourly jobs, summer jobs*

Temp Jobs
www.us.manpower.com
www.net-temps.com

Books
Cracking the Corporate Code: The Revealing Success Stories of 32 African-American Executives
by Price M. Cobbs and Judith L. Turnock

The authors surveyed 30 influential African-American executives to discuss their strategies for dealing with racial, cultural and organizational challenges.

Caught Between a Dream and a Job
by Delatorro McNeal II

Help readers to understand the process of transitioning from a great job to a great dream. Includes a "Discovering Your Purpose Inventory checklist."

Community organization that give back to young men

www.bbbs.org
Big Brothers Big Sisters

Help children reach their potential through professionally supported, one-to-one relationships with mentors that have a measurable impact on youth.

www.mentoring.org
MENTOR

For more than a decade, MENTOR/National Mentoring Partnership has been working to expand the world of quality mentoring. MENTOR believes that, with the help and guidance of an adult mentor, each child can discover how to unlock and achieve his or her potential.

www.100blackmen.org
100 Black Men of America, Inc.

Seeks to serve as a beacon of leadership by utilizing our diverse talents to create environments where our children are motivated to achieve, and to empower our people to become self-sufficient shareholders in the economic and social fabric of the communities we serve.

www.cbmnational.org
Concerned Black Men

Concerned Black Men CBM's vision is to fill the void of positive black male role models in many communities by providing mentors and programs that affirm the care and discipline that all youth need, while providing opportunities for academic and career enrichment. While the vision of CBM's founding members has expanded to include children and their parents nationwide, the philosophy of men offering themselves as positive role models to children has remained CBM's mission for more than 30 years.

www.stepstosuccess.org
The African American Male Initiative

Creating Success works to gain a better understanding of the issues facing young black males and to create new and better programs to address the needs of this vulnerable population.

www.bmcef.com
Black Male Community Empowerment Forum

A movement to save young Black men and to educate Black children

Resources for offenders/ex-offenders

www.exoffenderreentry.com
ExOffenderReentry.com

A one-stop resource center for corrections and re-entry success.

Books
Fighting for Your Life: The African-American Criminal Justice Survival Guide
by John Elmore

Teach how to choose the best attorney to help win your fight for justice; understand your rights and know what to do if you are arrested; survive if you get caught up in the criminal justice system; how to check your appearance and conduct in court to get the best possible outcome; everything you need to know about bail, juries and jail; how drugs and alcohol can lead to a life of crime and torment. How to make the right choices.

Steps to Finding a Job
for Ex-offenders on Parole

Step 1: Start your job search early. Don't wait until you are about to be released from prison.

Step 2: Search jobs that you have skill for, but check with employers to see what their policy is on hiring ex-offenders. Some jobs you will not be able to apply for.

Step 3: Stay on your parole officer to let them know you are searching for a job. They may be able to assist you in your search.

Step 4: Go to the US Department of Justice to find all jobs in your area that ex offenders are eligible for. This information can be found at any local library.

Step 5: American Civil Liberties Union should be contacted if you feel you are being mistreated. They will let you know what your rights are.

Step 6: If you are affiliated with a church in your area, find out what programs the church offers for ex-offenders. The Pastor may be able to assist you in your job search.

Step 7: Don't get discouraged and give up. Depending on your crime, it may be tough in the beginning to land employment, but it can happen if you continue to work hard and don't give up.

Step 8: Contact your parole officer to let them know the status of each of your job searches.

Fatherhood Initiatives

www.fatherhood.org
National Fatherhood Initiative

Improve the well being of children by increasing the proportion of children growing up with involved, responsible, and committed fathers.

www.fathers.com
National Center for Fathering

Improve the well-being of children by inspiring and equipping men to be more effectively involved in the lives of children.

http://fatherhood.hhs.gov
Promoting Responsible Fatherhood

This website contains links to fatherhood and related websites.

www.fathersnetwork.org
The Fathers Network

This site celebrates and supports fathers and families raising children with special health care needs and developmental disabilities.

www.cyfc.umn.edu/communities/programs/ftf.html
Father to Father

A national effort to unite men in the task of being a strong and positive force in their children's lives.

Abuse

www.helpguide.org

This site empower you and your loved ones to understand, prevent, and resolve health challenges such as abuse, addictions, anxiety, depression, stress and trauma.

www.saviorshope.org/dealing.php
Savior's Hope

A non-denominational Christian ministry that seeks to heal the wounds of men who were victims of childhood sexual abuse.

www.cyberparent.com/abuse

Discusses various forms of abuse.

Books
Healing the Shame That Binds You
by John Bradshaw

Focuses on "toxic shame": the feelings of hopelessness, worthlessness and inadequacy that many adult survivors of childhood sexual abuse carry into their adult lives. Bradshaw advocates getting this shame into the open, liberating the inner child, loving the self, awakening spiritually, and dealing more positively with relationships that reinforce the sense of toxic shame. He describes a number of strategies to help individuals move through a crippling sense of shame into greater self-acceptance.

I Will Survive: The African-American Guide to Healing from Sexual Assault and Abuse
by Lori Robinson

A valuable resource for African-American survivors of sexual assault (as well as their families, friends, and communities), incorporating personal stories, civil rights history, and a call for community activism.

Child Support

http://custodywarriors.blogspot.com
Blog devoted to fathers and husbands seeking custody of their children.

Books
Real Dads Stand Up!
by Alicia M. Crowe

A step-by-step easy to read guide which offers single fathers tips and legal insights about child support, parental rights, and custody.

The Emperor Penguin: A How to Guide for Fathers Wanting Custody of Their Kids
by J. M. Evans

A resource book for fathers attempting to get custody of their children.

Acknowledgments

First and foremost, I would like to thank my Lord and Savior Jesus Christ for his guidance through my ups and downs. God, you have brought me through so much and I owe all my success to you. I know I have failed many times and I thank you for second chances and for your forgiveness. I always complained about my biological father not being there, but you were always there for me and I thank you.

To my mother, Rosie A. Oliver, you were my mother and my father. You stuck by me through thick and thin since I was a kid and always supported me in everything that I have done. I thank you for being a role model to me and my sisters. You worked two and three jobs to take care of us. Even though you have been on dialysis for some 18 years now, you continue to fight despite the adversity you have gone through. I get my will to succeed from you. I love you mom.

To my deceased father Bobby Caulfield, even though I never met you, I inherited your ways and your looks. You missed out on something great, but I forgive you for not being there for me in my life. Whatever the reason is between you and God. May you rest in peace.

To my four sisters, Shirley, Barbara, Sandra and Michelle, I love each of you and thank you for your support.

To my extended family Tracy, Kim, Jalyn, Linda and Raymond Butler. Thanks for your continued support.

To all my nieces, nephews, cousins, uncles, aunts and extended family, far too many for me to name, but I thank you for your support.

To my children, Alyvia Rae Jackson and Robert Tye Jackson, you two are the light of your Daddy's life. I will always be there for you two no matter what.

I'm breaking the cycle. My father wasn't there for me, but your daddy will be there for you always. I love you both very much!

To my Pastor Dr. James Anthony Jackson, thanks for your encouraging sermons and words of wisdom. You have been a blessing to my life.

To my former pastors Jeffrey A. Johnson Sr. and Rev. Jonathon Bailey Sr. and to Rev. Dr. Stacy Spencer, Rev. Dr. Kevin W. Cosby thanks for your words of wisdom and inspiring sermons through the years. God bless you all.

To my best friend Dr. Sheila Thomas, I don't know if I could have made it through school without you. We went through some tough times growing up and I admire you for your strength when you lost your two oldest brothers. You have truly inspired me and you have always had my back. We have been friends over 25 years and I cherish our friendship.

To my boys Bill Miller, Keith Jones and Onaje Pinkney. You guys are like brothers to me.

To my God Parents, Bill and Leslie White, Jeanette Shotwell and "Mama" Marsha Smith thanks for your support through the years and I love all of you.

To my high school coach, Dave Enright, you pushed me to be the best that I could be and you brought the best out of me. Thanks for being there for me, coach.

To my college football coach, Jack Harbaugh, thanks for instilling that tough love in me at school both on and off the football field.

To my college roommates Eddie Godfrey and Melvin Johnson. Thanks for your friendship through the years.

To my childhood friends, Willie, Petey, Poncho, Kenny, Larry Shotwell (RIP), Tony Binion (RIP), Isaac, Herb Dove, Sherri and Terri Murray, Diane, Kenya, Debbie, Tricia, Orlando, Lalon, Ben, thanks for your friendship.

To Chere Cofer, Yolanda McTush, Retha Swain, Niquelle Allen and Sharon Wilson, thanks for your support of my work. To Steve Corbitt, Sean Gardner and David Gadis, you guys set the bar high, thanks for your friendship.

To Pamela Morrison. Thanks for giving a brother a chance after I left the NFL and thanks for helping to guide my career.

To my mentor Ralph Dowe, you bought my first suit and was the first real man I ever met. Even as an adult you instilled your knowledge in me. You spent your life changing the lives of others. Thank you for blessing my life and may you rest in peace.

To my brothers of Kappa Alpha Psi, Fraternity Inc., too many to name, Jeff Nixon, Sedrik Newbern, David Wilson, Craig Myers, Greg Monelle, Sam Watkins, Gene Murray, Carl Long, Anderson White and all the brothers of Epsilon Rho Chapter Western Kentucky University and the Indianapolis Alumni Chapter thanks for your continued support.

To Bud Myers, thanks for introducing me to 100 Black Men. To Ray Satterfield for the fatherly advice that you instilled in me over the past ten years. Thank you two for pushing me. I appreciate you both.

To my cousins Beverly and Chris and my Aunt Ann, thanks for welcoming me to my father's side of the family.

Special thanks to Center for Leadership Development, Kappa Alpha Psi, Fraternity Inc., National Pan-Hellenic Council, Inc., 100 Black Men of America, Indiana Black Expo, Indianapolis Housing Agency and Indianapolis Public Schools.

Finally, to my wife, friend, editor, publisher, Tajuana "TJ" Butler-Jackson, I couldn't have done this without you. You held down ten jobs to get this book done and encouraged me to write it. It was tough getting it done, but we did it and you helped me release so much. Thanks for inspiring me to talk about my past and face the demons of my father's absence and encouraging me to leave the excuses behind. God has truly blessed me with a strong, intelligent sister and I love you.

Robert Jackson

Robert Jackson, a Motivational Speaker and Trainer, is an award winning Specialty Rep with Teva Pharmaceuticals.

Robert received his BS, Industrial Technology degree from Western Kentucky University where he lettered four years in both football and track. A former Minnesota Vikings running back, Robert has remained deeply rooted in his commitment to serve his community. He speaks about issues concerning young black men, conflict resolution and fitness. Mr. Jackson is a member of Kappa Alpha Psi Fraternity, Inc., 100 Black Men of Indianapolis, National Sales Network (NSN), National Black MBA Association and the National Society of Black Engineers (NSBE). He mentors young men and has presented at several workshops and shares his message to both youth and adults all over the country.

Robert's motto is, *If you're not part of the solution, then you are part of the problem.*

If you are interested in learning more about Robert Jackson or if you want to book him to speak at your next event, please visit **www.blackmenstand.com**